Fix It Quick™

Favorite Brand Name™

BAKING

pil
Publications International, Ltd.
Favorite Brand Name Recipes at www.fbnr.com

Louis Weber, CEO
Publications International, Ltd.
7373 North Cicero Avenue
Lincolnwood, IL 60712

Pictured on the front cover: Ultimate Chocolate Chip Cookies *(page 34).*
Pictured on the back cover *(left to right):* Cheesecake Topped Brownies *(page 60),* Walnut-Orange Chocolate Chippers *(page 48)* and Chocolate Peanut Butter Cups *(page 98).*

ISBN: 1-4127-2237-3

Library of Congress Control Number: 2005924032

Manufactured in China.

8 7 6 5 4 3 2 1

Microwave Cooking: Microwave ovens vary in wattage. Use the cooking times as guidelines and check for doneness before adding more time.

Preparation/Cooking Times: Preparation times are based on the approximate amount of time required to assemble the recipe before cooking, baking, chilling or serving. These times include preparation steps such as measuring, chopping and mixing. The fact that some preparations and cooking can be done simultaneously is taken into account. Preparation of optional ingredients and serving suggestions is not included.

Contents

Basket of Breads

Cinnamon Bubble Ring

¼ cup sugar
½ teaspoon ground cinnamon
1 package (11 ounces) refrigerated French bread dough
1½ tablespoons butter or margarine, melted

1. Preheat oven to 350°F. Spray 9-inch tube pan with nonstick cooking spray. Combine sugar and cinnamon in small bowl.

2. Cut dough into 16 slices; roll into balls. Arrange 12 balls evenly spaced against outer wall of pan. Arrange remaining 4 balls evenly spaced against tube of pan. Brush with butter. Sprinkle sugar mixture evenly over balls.

3. Bake 20 to 25 minutes or until golden brown. Remove to serving plate. Serve warm.

Makes 8 servings

Tip: For a fast start to your morning, prepare the Cinnamon Bubble Ring in the pan the night before; cover and refrigerate. All you have to do in the morning is bake it for a quick, delicious treat.

Prep and Cook Time: 30 minutes

Cinnamon Bubble Ring

Orange Marmalade Bread

3 cups all-purpose flour
4 teaspoons baking powder
1 teaspoon salt
½ cup chopped walnuts
¾ cup milk
¾ cup SMUCKER'S® Orange Marmalade
2 eggs, lightly beaten
¼ cup honey
2 tablespoons CRISCO® Oil

Grease 9×5×3-inch loaf pan. Combine flour, baking powder and salt in large bowl. Stir in nuts. Combine milk, marmalade, eggs, honey and oil; blend well. Add to flour mixture; stir only until dry ingredients are moistened (batter will be lumpy). Turn into prepared pan.

Bake at 350°F for 65 to 70 minutes or until lightly browned and toothpick inserted in center comes out clean. *Makes 8 to 10 servings*

Coconut Date Nut Quick Bread

2 cups all-purpose flour
2 teaspoons baking powder
½ teaspoon baking soda
½ teaspoon salt
2 eggs
¾ cup thawed frozen unsweetened apple juice concentrate
¼ cup (½ stick) butter, melted
¼ cup fat-free (skim) milk
2 teaspoons vanilla
1 cup chopped pitted dates
½ cup chopped walnuts or pecans
⅓ cup unsweetened flaked coconut*
Cream cheese (optional)

**Unsweetened flaked coconut is available in health food stores.*

Preheat oven to 350°F. Grease 9×5-inch loaf pan. Combine dry ingredients in medium bowl; set aside. Beat eggs in separate medium bowl. Blend in apple juice concentrate, butter, milk and vanilla. Add to dry ingredients; mix just until moistened. Stir in dates, walnuts and coconut. Spread into prepared loaf pan. Bake 45 minutes or until toothpick inserted in center comes out clean. Cool 10 minutes in pan on wire rack. Remove from pan; cool completely. Slice and serve at room temperature, or toast slices and spread with cream cheese, if desired.

Makes 12 servings

Orange Marmalade Bread

Corn Bread

1 cup all-purpose flour
1 cup yellow cornmeal
⅓ cup sugar
2 teaspoons baking powder
½ teaspoon salt
1 cup milk
⅓ cup vegetable oil
1 egg

1. Preheat oven to 400°F. Grease 8-inch square baking pan.

2. Combine flour, cornmeal, sugar, baking powder and salt in large bowl; set aside. Combine milk, oil and egg in small bowl until blended. Stir milk mixture into flour mixture just until moistened. Spread batter evenly in prepared pan.

3. Bake 20 to 25 minutes or until golden brown and toothpick inserted in center comes out clean. Cut into squares. Serve warm. *Makes 9 servings*

Corn Muffins: Preheat oven to 400°F. Prepare batter as directed in step 2, except spoon batter into 12 (2½-inch) greased or paper-lined muffin pan cups. Bake 20 minutes or until golden brown and toothpicks inserted into centers come out clean. Immediately remove from pan; cool on wire rack 10 minutes. Serve warm. Makes 12 muffins.

Corn Sticks: Preheat oven to 425°F. Heat cast-iron corn stick pan in oven while preparing batter as directed in step 2. Carefully brush hot pan with additional vegetable oil before spooning half of batter into prepared pan. Bake 10 to 15 minutes or until lightly browned. Immediately remove from pan; cool on wire racks 10 minutes. Repeat with remaining half of batter. Serve warm. Makes 14 corn sticks.

Popovers

1 cup all-purpose flour
1 cup milk
3 eggs
1 tablespoon butter, at room temperature
½ teaspoon salt

1. Heat oven to 375°F. Grease and flour 12 muffin cups or six 6-ounce custard cups.

2. Fit processor with steel blade. Add all ingredients to work bowl. Process 2½ minutes continuously.

3. Pour batter into prepared cups, filling each about ¾ full. Bake 45 to 50 minutes or until dark brown and crispy. Serve immediately.

Makes 12 small or 6 large popovers

Cheese Popovers: Prepare batter as directed for Popovers, substituting ½ teaspoon garlic salt for salt. After processing batter, stop processor and add ½ cup shredded Cheddar or Swiss cheese to batter. Process on/off twice to mix. Pour batter into cups and bake as above.

Corn Bread, Corn Muffins and Corn Sticks

German Rye Beer Bread

1½-Pound Loaf

1¼ cups light beer, at room temperature
2 tablespoons light molasses
1 tablespoon butter
1½ teaspoons salt
2½ cups bread flour
½ cup rye flour
2 teaspoons caraway seeds
1½ teaspoons rapid-rise active dry yeast

2-Pound Loaf

1½ cups light beer, at room temperature
3 tablespoons light molasses
1½ tablespoons butter
2 teaspoons salt
3¼ cups bread flour
¾ cup rye flour
1 tablespoon caraway seeds
2 teaspoons rapid-rise active dry yeast

Bread Machine Directions

1. Measuring carefully, place all ingredients in bread machine pan in order specified by owner's manual.

2. Program basic cycle and desired crust setting; press start. Remove baked bread from pan; cool on wire rack. *Makes 12 or 16 servings (1 loaf)*

Fruited Oat Scones

1½ cups all-purpose flour
1¼ cups QUAKER® Oats (quick or old fashioned, uncooked)
¼ cup granulated sugar
1 tablespoon baking powder
¼ teaspoon salt (optional)
⅓ cup (5⅓ tablespoons) margarine
1⅓ cups (6-ounce package) diced dried mixed fruit
½ cup milk
1 egg, lightly beaten
1 teaspoon granulated sugar
⅛ teaspoon ground cinnamon

Preheat oven to 375°F. Combine flour, oats, ¼ cup sugar, baking powder and salt; mix well. Cut in margarine with pastry blender or two knives until mixture resembles coarse crumbs; stir in fruit. Add milk and egg, mixing just until moistened. Shape dough into ball. Turn out onto floured surface; knead gently 6 times. On lightly greased cookie sheet, pat out dough to form 8-inch circle. With sharp knife, score round into 12 wedges; sprinkle with combined 1 teaspoon sugar and cinnamon. Bake about 30 minutes or until golden brown. Break apart; serve warm.

Makes 1 dozen scones

German Rye Beer Bread

Fast Pesto Focaccia

1 can (10 ounces) refrigerated pizza crust dough
2 tablespoons prepared pesto
4 sun-dried tomatoes (packed in oil), drained

1. Preheat oven to 425°F. Lightly grease 8×8×2-inch pan. Unroll pizza dough. Fold in half; pat into pan.

2. Spread pesto evenly over dough. Chop tomatoes or snip with kitchen scissors; sprinkle over pesto. Press tomatoes into dough. Using wooden spoon handle, make indentations in dough every 2 inches.

3. Bake 10 to 12 minutes or until golden brown. Cut into 16 squares and serve warm or at room temperature. *Makes 16 servings*

Prep and Cook Time: 20 minutes

Orange Breakfast Loaf

1 cup water
⅓ cup orange juice
2 tablespoons vegetable oil
1 teaspoon salt
2 cups all-purpose flour
1 cup old-fashioned oats
1 cup whole wheat flour
½ cup dried cranberries
2 tablespoons sugar
1 teaspoon freshly grated orange peel
2 teaspoons active dry yeast

Bread Machine Directions

1. Measuring carefully, place all ingredients in bread machine pan in order specified by owner's manual.

2. Program basic or white cycle and desired crust setting; press start. Remove baked bread from pan; cool on wire rack.

Makes 1 (1½-pound) loaf (12 to 16 servings)

Quick Tip

Let a freshly baked loaf of bread cool for at least three hours on a wire rack before freezing. Place the loaf in the freezer on a flat surface for two hours or until it is completely frozen. Wrap the frozen loaf in plastic wrap, then in heavy-duty aluminum foil. Label it with the date and the type of bread and return it to the freezer. Bread can be frozen for up to six months. Thaw the frozen bread in its wrapping at room temperature for two to three hours. You can freshen the loaf by heating it in a 300°F oven for 20 minutes.

Fast Pesto Focaccia

Apricot Holiday Bread

⅔ cup milk
1 egg
2 tablespoons butter, softened
1 teaspoon salt
3 cups all-purpose flour
½ cup pecan or walnut pieces
½ cup dried apricots or peaches, chopped
2 tablespoons sugar
¼ teaspoon ground ginger
¼ teaspoon ground nutmeg
1 tablespoon active dry yeast

Bread Machine Directions

1. Measuring carefully, place all ingredients in bread machine pan in order specified by owner's manual.

2. Program basic or white cycle and desired crust setting; press start. (Do not use delay cycle.) Remove baked bread from pan; cool on wire rack.

Makes 1 (1½-*pound*) *loaf* (12 *to* 16 *servings*)

Gannat (French Cheese Bread)

2 eggs
3 tablespoons water
¼ cup (½ stick) butter or margarine, cut up and softened
1 teaspoon salt
2½ cups all-purpose flour
1 cup (4 ounces) shredded Cheddar or Swiss cheese
1 teaspoon sugar
2 teaspoons active dry yeast

Bread Machine Directions

1. Measuring carefully, place all ingredients in bread machine pan in order specified by owner's manual.

2. Program basic or white cycle and desired crust setting; press start. (Do not use delay cycle.) Remove baked bread from pan; cool on wire rack.

Makes 1 (1½-*pound*) *loaf* (12 *to* 16 *servings*)

Apricot Holiday Bread

Hawaiian Fruit and Nut Quick Bread

2 cups all-purpose flour
1 tablespoon orange-flavored instant drink powder
2 teaspoons baking soda
1 teaspoon cinnamon
¾ cup granulated sugar
¾ cup light brown sugar
¾ cup chopped macadamia nuts
½ cup shredded coconut
¾ cup canola oil
2 eggs
2 teaspoons rum extract
2 cups chopped fresh mango

1. Preheat oven to 350°F. Lightly grease 9×3-inch loaf pan. Set aside.

2. Sift flour, drink powder, baking soda and cinnamon into medium bowl. Stir in sugars, macadamia nuts and coconut. Combine oil, eggs and rum extract in separate medium bowl. Add to dry mixture; stir to mix well. Stir in mango.

3. Spoon batter into prepared pan. Bake 60 to 70 minutes or until bread is light golden brown and pulls away from sides of pan. Cool in pan 10 minutes. Remove to wire rack and cool completely.

Makes 1 loaf

Clover Tea Rolls

2 cups sifted all-purpose flour
¼ cup sugar
¾ teaspoon Arm & Hammer® Baking Soda
½ teaspoon salt
⅓ cup vegetable shortening
½ cup milk
3 tablespoons lemon juice

Sift together flour, sugar, baking soda and salt into large bowl. Cut in shortening until mixture resembles coarse meal. Combine milk and lemon juice; quickly stir into flour mixture to form a soft dough.

Turn dough onto lightly floured board; knead slightly. Form into 36 small balls about the size of marbles. Place three balls into each greased muffin cup (about 2¼-inch diameter). Bake in 450°F oven 15 minutes or until lightly browned.

Makes about 1 dozen rolls

Hawaiian Fruit and Nut Quick Bread

Original Ranch® & Cheddar Bread

1 cup HIDDEN VALLEY® The Original Ranch® Dressing
2 cups (8 ounces) shredded sharp Cheddar cheese
1 whole loaf (1 pound) French bread (not sour dough)

Stir together dressing and cheese. Cut bread in half lengthwise. Place on a broiler pan and spread dressing mixture evenly over cut side of each half. Broil until lightly brown. Cut each half into 8 pieces. *Makes 16 pieces*

Sticky Buns

24 frozen bread dough rolls, thawed
1 package (4-serving size) butterscotch cook-and-serve pudding and pie filling mix (not instant)
½ cup firmly packed brown sugar
½ cup chopped pecans
½ cup (1 stick) butter or margarine, melted

1. Grease 12-cup Bundt pan. Layer rolls in pan. Sprinkle pudding mix, brown sugar and pecans over rolls. Drizzle butter on top. Cover pan with foil and refrigerate overnight.

2. Preheat oven to 400°F. Remove foil and bake 20 minutes or until lightly browned. Invert rolls onto serving plate. *Makes 24 servings*

Tip: Place a baking sheet underneath Bundt pan while baking to catch drippings.

Country Biscuits

2 cups all-purpose flour
1 tablespoon baking powder
1 teaspoon salt
⅓ CRISCO® Stick or ⅓ cup CRISCO® all-vegetable shortening
¾ cup milk

1. Heat oven to 425°F. Combine flour, baking powder and salt in medium bowl. Cut in ⅓ cup shortening using pastry blender (or two knives) to form coarse crumbs. Add milk. Mix with fork until dry mixture is moistened. Form dough into a ball.

2. Transfer dough to lightly floured surface. Knead gently 8 to 10 times. Roll out dough to ½-inch thickness. Cut with floured 2-inch round cutter. Place on ungreased baking sheet.

3. Bake at 425°F for 12 to 14 minutes or until golden. *Do not overbake.* *Makes 12 to 16 biscuits*

Original Ranch® & Cheddar Bread

Herb Cheese Twists

- **2 tablespoons butter or margarine**
- **¼ cup grated Parmesan cheese**
- **1 teaspoon dried parsley flakes**
- **1 teaspoon dried basil leaves**
- **1 can (7½ ounces) refrigerated buttermilk biscuits**

1. Preheat oven to 400°F. Lightly grease baking sheet. Microwave butter in small bowl at MEDIUM (50% power) just until melted; cool slightly. Stir in cheese, parsley and basil. Set aside.

2. Pat each biscuit into 5×2-inch rectangle. Spread 1 teaspoon butter mixture onto each rectangle; cut each in half lengthwise. Twist each strip 3 or 4 times. Place on prepared baking sheet. Bake 8 to 10 minutes or until golden brown. *Makes 5 servings*

Variation: Save even more time by using ready-to-bake breadsticks. Spread the butter mixture onto the breadsticks, then bake them according to the package directions.

Prep and Cook Time: 20 minutes

Potato Bread

1½-Pound Loaf

- **1⅓ cups water**
- **1½ tablespoons margarine or butter**
- **1½ teaspoons salt**
- **3 cups bread flour**
- **½ cup mashed potato flakes**
- **2 tablespoons sugar**
- **2 tablespoons nonfat dry milk powder**
- **1½ teaspoons rapid-rise active dry yeast**

2-Pound Loaf

- **1¾ cups water**
- **2 tablespoons margarine or butter**
- **2 teaspoons salt**
- **4 cups bread flour**
- **¾ cup mashed potato flakes**
- **3 tablespoons sugar**
- **3 tablespoons nonfat dry milk powder**
- **2 teaspoons rapid-rise active dry yeast**

Bread Machine Directions

1. Measuring carefully, place all ingredients in bread machine pan in order specified by owner's manual.

2. Program basic cycle and desired crust setting; press start. Remove baked bread from pan; cool on wire rack. *Makes 12 or 16 servings*

Serving Suggestion: Serve with a homemade herb butter. To make, combine ½ cup softened butter and 1 tablespoon of your favorite chopped fresh herbs in a small bowl.

Herb Cheese Twists

Quick Corn Bread with Chilies 'n' Cheese

- 1 package (12 to 16 ounces) corn bread or corn muffin mix
- 1 cup (4 ounces) shredded Monterey Jack cheese, divided
- 1 can (4 ounces) chopped green chilies, drained
- 1 envelope LIPTON® RECIPE SECRETS® Vegetable Soup Mix

Prepare corn bread mix according to package directions; stir in ½ cup cheese, chilies and vegetable soup mix. Pour batter into lightly greased 8-inch baking pan; bake as directed. While warm, top with remaining ½ cup cheese. Cool completely on wire rack. To serve, cut into squares. *Makes 16 servings*

Spicy Onion Bread

- 2 tablespoons instant minced onion
- ⅓ cup water
- 1½ cups biscuit mix
- 1 egg, lightly beaten
- ½ cup milk
- ½ teaspoon TABASCO® brand Pepper Sauce
- 2 tablespoons butter, melted
- ½ teaspoon caraway seeds (optional)

Preheat oven to 400°F. Soak instant minced onion in water 5 minutes. Combine biscuit mix, egg, milk and TABASCO® Sauce in large bowl and stir until blended. Stir in onion. Turn into greased 8-inch pie plate. Brush with melted butter. Sprinkle with caraway seeds. Bake 20 to 25 minutes or until golden brown. *Makes 8 servings*

Honey of a Whole Wheat Bread

1-Pound Loaf

- ¼ cup water
- ¼ cup milk
- 1 large egg, at room temperature
- 2 tablespoons honey
- 2 teaspoons butter, cut into small pieces
- 1½ teaspoons salt
- ⅔ cup whole wheat flour
- 1⅓ cups bread flour
- 1½ teaspoons RED STAR® Active Dry Yeast or 1 teaspoon QUICK•RISE™ Yeast or Bread Machine Yeast

1½-Pound Loaf

- ¼ cup water
- ½ cup milk
- 1 large egg, at room temperature
- ¼ cup honey
- 1 tablespoon butter, cut into small pieces
- 2 teaspoons salt
- 1 cup whole wheat flour
- 2 cups bread flour
- 2¼ teaspoons (1 packet) RED STAR® Active Dry Yeast or 1½ teaspoons QUICK•RISE™ Yeast or Bread Machine Yeast

Bread Machine Directions

Place room temperature ingredients in pan in order listed. Select basic/white cycle, medium crust. Do not use delay timer. Check dough consistency after 5 minutes of kneading making adjustment, if necessary. Cool on rack. *Makes 1 loaf*

Quick Corn Bread with Chilies 'n' Cheese

Mediterranean Bread Braid

- 2 teaspoons dried basil leaves
- 1 teaspoon dried oregano leaves
- ½ teaspoon dried rosemary leaves
- ¼ teaspoon garlic powder
- 1 package (11 ounces) refrigerated French bread dough
- 2 ounces olives, pitted and finely chopped (about 16)
- 2 teaspoons olive oil

1. Preheat oven to 350°F.

2. Combine basil, oregano, rosemary and garlic powder in small bowl.

3. Lightly spray baking sheet with nonstick cooking spray. Place dough roll on baking sheet; unroll. Sprinkle evenly with olives and basil mixture. Cut lengthwise into 3 strips. Fold each strip in half lengthwise, creating 3 rope-like strips. Braid bread and tuck ends under slightly.

4. Bake 26 minutes or until bread is golden and sounds hollow when lightly tapped.

5. Remove from oven; place on cutting board to cool. Brush olive oil over top. Cut diagonally into 12 slices. *Makes 12 servings (1 loaf)*

Tip: Peak flavors are reached by allowing the bread to cool to room temperature.

Prep Time: 10 minutes
Bake Time: 26 minutes
Cool Time: About 1 hour

Crispy Ranch Breadsticks

- 2 tablespoons dry ranch party dip mix
- 2 tablespoons sour cream
- 1 package (10 ounces) refrigerated pizza dough
- Butter, melted

1. Preheat oven to 400°F. Grease baking sheets or line with parchment paper. Combine dip mix and sour cream in small bowl; set aside.

2. Unroll pizza dough on lightly floured work surface. Shape dough into 16×10-inch rectangle. Brush with melted butter. Spread dip mixture evenly over top of dough; cut into 24 (10-inch) strips. Form into desired shapes.

3. Place breadsticks ½ inch apart on prepared baking sheets. Bake 10 minutes or until golden brown. Serve immediately or place on wire rack to cool. *Makes 24 breadsticks*

Crispy Spiced Nut Breadsticks: Place 1 cup finely chopped pecans and 1 tablespoon vegetable oil in plastic bag; toss to coat. Combine ¼ teaspoon chili powder, ¼ teaspoon ground cumin, ¼ teaspoon curry powder, ⅛ teaspoon ground cinnamon and dash of ground red pepper in small bowl. Add to nuts; toss to coat. Place nuts in small pan over medium heat and stir constantly until nuts are lightly toasted. Sprinkle nut mixture with 1 teaspoon garlic salt; cool to room temperature. Instead of spreading dough with sour cream mixture, sprinkle ½ cup spiced nuts over dough (store remaining nuts in tightly covered container). Cut into 24 (10-inch) strips. Form into desired shapes. Bake as directed. Makes 24 breadsticks.

Mediterranean Bread Braid

Walnut-Chocolate Quick Bread

1½ cups milk
1 cup sugar
⅓ cup vegetable oil
1 egg, beaten
1 tablespoon molasses
1 teaspoon vanilla
3 cups all-purpose flour
3 tablespoons unsweetened cocoa powder
2 teaspoons baking soda
2 teaspoons baking powder
1 teaspoon salt
1 cup chocolate chips
½ cup walnuts, coarsely chopped

1. Preheat oven to 350°F. Grease four 5×3-inch loaf pans; set aside.

2. Combine milk, sugar, oil, egg, molasses and vanilla in medium bowl. Stir until sugar is dissolved.

3. Combine flour, cocoa, baking soda, baking powder and salt in large bowl. Add chocolate chips, walnuts and milk mixture; stir just until combined. Pour into prepared pans.

4. Bake 30 minutes or until toothpicks inserted into centers of loaves come out clean. Cool in pans 15 minutes. Remove from pans and cool on wire racks. *Makes 4 small loaves*

Muffin Variation: Preheat oven to 375°F. Spoon batter into 12 greased muffin cups. Bake 20 minutes or until toothpicks inserted into centers come out clean. Makes 12 muffins.

Soda Bread

1½ cups whole wheat flour
1 cup all-purpose flour
½ cup rolled oats
¼ cup sugar
1½ teaspoons baking powder
½ teaspoon baking soda
¼ teaspoon ground cinnamon
⅓ cup raisins (optional)
¼ cup walnuts (optional)
1¼ cups low-fat buttermilk
1 tablespoon vegetable oil

Preheat oven to 375°F. Combine whole wheat flour, all-purpose flour, oats, sugar, baking powder, baking soda and cinnamon in large bowl. Stir in raisins and walnuts, if desired. Gradually stir in buttermilk and oil until dough forms. Knead in bowl for 30 seconds. Spray 8×4-inch loaf pan with nonstick cooking spray; place dough in pan. Bake 40 to 50 minutes or until wooden toothpick inserted into center comes out clean. *Makes 16 slices*

Favorite recipe from **The Sugar Association, Inc.**

Walnut-Chocolate Quick Bread

Honey Wheat Bread

½ cup water
3 tablespoons honey
1 egg
2 tablespoons butter or margarine, softened
1 teaspoon salt
2 cups all-purpose flour
¾ cup whole wheat flour
¼ cup nonfat dry milk powder
2 teaspoons active dry yeast

Bread Machine Directions

1. Measuring carefully, place all ingredients in bread machine pan in order specified by owner's manual.

2. Program basic or white cycle and desired crust setting; press start. (Do not use delay cycle.) Remove baked bread from pan; cool on wire rack.

Makes 1 (1-pound) loaf

Quick Tip

Salt adds flavor to breads and also controls the action of the yeast. It slows the rising time, allowing the flavors of the dough to develop. Salt also strengthens the gluten, thus contributing to the texture.

Sesame Italian Breadsticks

¼ cup grated Parmesan cheese
3 tablespoons sesame seeds
2 teaspoons dried Italian seasoning
1 teaspoon kosher salt (optional)
12 frozen bread dough dinner rolls, thawed
¼ cup (½ stick) butter, melted

1. Preheat oven to 425°F. Spray large baking sheet with nonstick cooking spray.

2. Combine cheese, sesame seeds, Italian seasoning and salt, if desired, in small bowl. Spread out on plate.

3. Roll each dinner roll into rope, about 8 inches long and ½ inch thick, on lightly floured surface; place on baking sheet. Brush tops and sides with butter. Roll each buttered rope in cheese mixture, pressing mixture into dough. Return ropes to baking sheet, placing 2 inches apart. Twist each rope 3 times. Press both ends of rope down on baking sheet. Bake 10 to 12 minutes or until golden brown.

Makes 12 breadsticks

Honey Wheat Bread

Cookie Extravaganza

Mini Pizza Cookies

1 20-ounce tube refrigerated sugar cookie dough
2 cups (16 ounces) prepared pink frosting
"M&M's"® Chocolate Mini Baking Bits
Variety of additional toppings such as shredded coconut, granola, raisins, nuts, small pretzels, snack mixes, sunflower seeds, popped corn and mini marshmallows

Preheat oven to 350°F. Lightly grease cookie sheets; set aside. Divide dough into 8 equal portions. On lightly floured surface, roll each portion of dough into ¼-inch-thick circle; place circles about 2 inches apart onto prepared cookie sheets. Bake 10 to 13 minutes or until golden brown on edges. Cool completely on wire racks. Spread top of each pizza with frosting; sprinkle with "M&M's"® Chocolate Mini Baking Bits and 2 or 3 suggested toppings. *Makes 8 cookies*

Mini Pizza Cookies

Double Chocolate Oat Cookies

2 cups (12 ounces) semisweet chocolate pieces, divided
½ cup (1 stick) margarine or butter, softened
½ cup granulated sugar
1 egg
¼ teaspoon vanilla
¾ cup all-purpose flour
¾ cup QUAKER® Oats (quick or old fashioned, uncooked)
1 teaspoon baking powder
¼ teaspoon baking soda
¼ teaspoon salt (optional)

Preheat oven to 375°F. Melt 1 cup chocolate pieces in small saucepan; set aside. Beat margarine and sugar until fluffy; add melted chocolate, egg and vanilla. Add combined flour, oats, baking powder, baking soda and salt; mix well. Stir in remaining chocolate pieces. Drop by rounded tablespoonfuls onto *ungreased* cookie sheets. Bake 8 to 10 minutes. Cool 1 minute on cookie sheets; remove to wire racks.

Makes about 3 dozen cookies

Easy Lemon Cookies

1 package DUNCAN HINES® Moist Deluxe® Lemon Cake Mix
2 eggs
½ cup vegetable oil
1 teaspoon grated lemon peel
Pecan halves for garnish

1. Preheat oven to 350°F.

2. Combine cake mix, eggs, oil and lemon peel in large bowl. Stir until well blended. Drop by rounded teaspoonfuls 2 inches apart onto ungreased baking sheets. Press pecan half into center of each cookie. Bake at 350°F for 9 to 11 minutes or until edges are light golden brown. Cool 1 minute on baking sheets. Remove to wire racks. Cool completely. Store in airtight container.

Makes 4 dozen cookies

Tip: You can substitute whole almonds or walnut halves for the pecan halves.

Double Chocolate Oat Cookies

Ultimate Chocolate Chip Cookies

1¼ cups firmly packed brown sugar
¾ Butter Flavor CRISCO® Stick or ¾ cup Butter Flavor CRISCO® all-vegetable shortening
2 tablespoons milk
1 tablespoon vanilla
1 egg
1¾ cups all-purpose flour
1 teaspoon salt
¾ teaspoon baking soda
1 cup semisweet chocolate chips
1 cup coarsely chopped pecans*

**You can substitute an additional ½ cup semisweet chocolate chips for pecans.*

1. Heat oven to 375°F. Place sheets of foil on countertop for cooling cookies.

2. Combine sugar, ¾ cup shortening, milk and vanilla in large bowl. Beat at medium speed of electric mixer until well blended. Beat in egg.

3. Combine flour, salt and baking soda. Mix into shortening mixture at low speed just until blended. Stir in chocolate chips and nuts.

4. Drop by rounded tablespoonfuls 3 inches apart onto ungreased baking sheets.

5. Bake at 375°F for 8 to 10 minutes for chewy cookies or 11 to 13 minutes for crisp cookies. *Do not overbake.* Cool 2 minutes on baking sheets. Remove to foil to cool completely.

Makes about 3 dozen cookies

Drizzle: Combine 1 teaspoon Butter Flavor CRISCO® and 1 cup semisweet chocolate chips or 1 cup white melting chocolate, cut into small pieces, in microwave-safe measuring cup. Microwave at 50% (MEDIUM). Stir after 1 minute. Repeat until smooth (or melt on rangetop in small saucepan on very low heat). To thin, add more Butter Flavor Crisco®. Drizzle back and forth over cookies. Sprinkle with nuts before chocolate hardens, if desired. To quickly harden chocolate, place cookies in refrigerator to set.

Chocolate Dipped: Melt chocolate as directed for Drizzle. Dip half of cooled cookies in chocolate. Sprinkle with finely chopped nuts before chocolate hardens. Place on waxed paper until chocolate is firm. To quickly harden chocolate, place cookies in refrigerator to set.

Flourless Peanut Butter Cookies

1 cup peanut butter
1 cup packed light brown sugar
1 egg
24 milk chocolate candy stars or milk chocolate candy kisses

1. Preheat oven to 350°F. Combine peanut butter, sugar and egg in medium bowl; beat until blended and smooth.

2. Shape dough into 24 balls about 1½ inches in diameter. Place 2 inches apart on ungreased cookie sheets. Press one chocolate star on top of each cookie. Bake 10 to 12 minutes or until set. Transfer to wire racks to cool completely.

Makes about 2 dozen cookies

Ultimate Chocolate Chip Cookies

Strawberry Hearts

1 roll (17 to 18 ounces) refrigerated sugar cookie dough
2 packages (8 ounces each) cream cheese, softened
⅔ cup powdered sugar
1 teaspoon vanilla
2 cups sliced fresh strawberries

1. Remove dough from wrapper. Roll out dough, cut out hearts and bake as directed on package.

2. Combine cream cheese, powdered sugar and vanilla; mix well.

3. Spread evenly onto cooled hearts; top evenly with strawberries. *Makes about 2 dozen hearts*

Peanut Butter Chip Pineapple Drops

¼ cup (½ stick) butter or margarine, softened
¼ cup shortening
1 cup packed light brown sugar
1 egg
1 teaspoon vanilla extract
2 cups all-purpose flour
1 teaspoon baking powder
½ teaspoon baking soda
½ teaspoon salt
1 can (8 ounces) crushed pineapple, drained
1 cup REESE'S® Peanut Butter Chips
½ cup chopped nuts (optional)
Red candied cherries, halved

1. Heat oven to 375°F.

2. Beat butter and shortening in large bowl until blended. Add sugar, egg and vanilla; beat until fluffy. Stir together flour, baking powder, baking soda and salt; add to butter mixture, beating until well blended. Stir in pineapple, peanut butter chips and nuts, if desired. Drop by teaspoons onto ungreased cookie sheet. Lightly press cherry half in center of each cookie.

3. Bake 10 to 12 minutes or until lightly browned. Remove from cookie sheet to wire rack. Cool completely. *Makes about 3½ dozen cookies*

Strawberry Hearts

Chocolate Chip Macaroons

2½ cups flaked coconut
⅔ cup mini semisweet chocolate chips
⅔ cup sweetened condensed milk
1 teaspoon vanilla

1. Preheat oven to 350°F. Grease cookie sheets. Combine coconut, chocolate chips, milk and vanilla in medium bowl; mix until well blended.

2. Drop dough by rounded teaspoonfuls 2 inches apart onto prepared cookie sheets. Press dough gently with back of spoon to flatten slightly. Bake 10 to 12 minutes or until light golden brown. Let cookies stand on cookie sheets 1 minute. Remove cookies to wire racks; cool completely.

Makes about 3½ dozen cookies

Quick Tip

A cookie with a crisp, yet chewy texture, a macaroon is traditionally made from egg whites and sugar and flavored with ground almonds or almond paste. A variation with coconut substituted for almonds is almost more popular than the original. Chocolate and cherries are also sometimes added to macaroons.

Quick Fruit & Lemon Drops

1 package (about 18 ounces) lemon cake mix
⅓ cup water
¼ cup (½ stick) butter, softened
1 egg
1 tablespoon grated lemon peel
1 cup mixed dried fruit bits
½ cup sugar

1. Preheat oven to 350°F. Grease cookie sheets.

2. Beat cake mix, water, butter, egg and lemon peel in large bowl with electric mixer at low speed until well blended. Beat in fruit bits just until blended.

3. Place sugar in shallow bowl. Shape dough by heaping tablespoons into balls; roll in sugar. Place 2 inches apart on prepared cookie sheets.

4. Bake 12 to 14 minutes or until set. Cool on cookie sheets 2 minutes. Transfer to wire racks; cool completely.

Makes about 2 dozen cookies

Note: If dough is too sticky add about ¼ cup all-purpose flour.

Chocolate Chip Macaroons

Coconut Clouds

- 2⅔ cups flaked coconut, divided
- 1 package DUNCAN HINES® Moist Deluxe® Classic Yellow Cake Mix
- 1 egg
- ½ cup vegetable oil
- ¼ cup water
- 1 teaspoon almond extract

1. Preheat oven to 350°F. Reserve 1⅓ cups coconut in medium bowl.

2. Combine cake mix, egg, oil, water and almond extract in large bowl. Beat at low speed with electric mixer. Stir in remaining 1⅓ cups coconut. Drop rounded teaspoonful of dough into reserved coconut. Roll to cover lightly. Place on ungreased baking sheet. Repeat with remaining dough, placing balls 2 inches apart. Bake at 350°F for 10 to 12 minutes or until light golden brown. Cool 1 minute on baking sheets. Remove to cooling racks. Cool completely. Store in airtight container. *Makes 3½ dozen cookies*

Hint: To save time when forming dough into balls, use a 1-inch spring-operated cookie scoop. Spring-operated cookie scoops are available at kitchen specialty shops.

White Chip Apricot Oatmeal Cookies

- ¾ cup (1½ sticks) butter or margarine, softened
- ½ cup granulated sugar
- ½ cup packed light brown sugar
- 2 eggs
- 1 cup all-purpose flour
- 1 teaspoon baking soda
- 2½ cups rolled oats
- 2 cups (12-ounce package) HERSHEY®S Premier White Chips
- 1 cup chopped dried apricots

1. Heat oven to 375°F.

2. Beat butter, granulated sugar and brown sugar in large bowl until fluffy. Add egg; beat well. Add flour and baking soda; beat until well blended. Stir in oats, white chips and apricots. Loosely form rounded teaspoonfuls dough into balls; place on ungreased cookie sheet.

3. Bake 7 to 9 minutes or just until lightly browned; do not overbake. Cool 1 to 2 minutes; remove from cookie sheet to wire rack. Cool completely. *Makes about 3½ dozen cookies*

Coconut Clouds

Choc-Oat-Chip Cookies

- 1 cup (2 sticks) butter or margarine, softened
- 1 cup firmly packed brown sugar
- ½ cup granulated sugar
- 2 eggs
- 2 tablespoons milk
- 2 teaspoons vanilla
- 1¾ cups all-purpose flour
- 1 teaspoon baking soda
- ½ teaspoon salt (optional)
- 2½ cups QUAKER® Oats (quick or old fashioned, uncooked)
- 2 cups semisweet chocolate pieces
- 1 cup coarsely chopped nuts (optional)

Preheat oven to 375°F. Beat together butter and sugars until creamy. Add eggs, milk and vanilla; beat well. Add combined flour, baking soda and salt; mix well. Stir in oats, chocolate pieces and nuts; mix well. Drop by rounded tablespoonfuls onto ungreased cookie sheets.* Bake at 375°F for 9 to 10 minutes for a chewy cookie or 12 to 13 minutes for a crisp cookie. Cool 1 minute on cookie sheets; remove to wire racks. Cool completely. Store in tightly covered container.

Makes about 5 dozen cookies

**For bar cookies:* Press dough evenly into ungreased 13×9-inch metal baking pan. Bake 30 to 35 minutes or until light golden brown. Cool completely; cut into bars. Store tightly covered.*

High altitude adjustment: Increase flour to 2 cups.

Variations: Prepare cookies as recipe directs, except substitute 1 cup of any of the following for 1 cup chocolate pieces: raisins; chopped dried apricots; dried cherries; crushed toffee pieces; candy-coated chocolate pieces; white chocolate baking pieces.

Honey Spice Balls

- ½ cup (1 stick) butter, softened
- ½ cup packed brown sugar
- 1 egg
- 1 tablespoon honey
- 1 teaspoon vanilla
- 2 cups all-purpose flour
- ½ teaspoon baking powder
- ½ teaspoon ground cinnamon
- ¼ teaspoon ground nutmeg
- Uncooked quick oats

1. Preheat oven to 350°F. Grease cookie sheets. Beat butter and brown sugar in large bowl with electric mixer until creamy. Add egg, honey and vanilla; beat until light and fluffy. Stir in flour, baking powder, cinnamon and nutmeg until well blended. Shape tablespoonfuls of dough into balls; roll in oats. Place 2 inches apart on prepared cookie sheets.

2. Bake 15 to 18 minutes or until cookie tops crack slightly. Cool 1 minute on cookie sheets. Remove to wire racks; cool completely. Store in airtight container. *Makes about 2½ dozen cookies*

Spicy Lemon Crescents

- 1 cup (2 sticks) butter or margarine, softened
- 1½ cups powdered sugar, divided
- ½ teaspoon lemon extract
- ½ teaspoon grated lemon zest
- 2 cups cake flour
- ½ cup finely chopped almonds, walnuts or pecans
- 1 teaspoon ground cinnamon
- ½ teaspoon ground cardamom
- ½ teaspoon ground nutmeg
- 1¾ cups "M&M's"® Chocolate Mini Baking Bits

Preheat oven to 375°F. Lightly grease cookie sheets; set aside. In large bowl cream butter and ½ cup sugar; add lemon extract and zest until well blended. In medium bowl combine flour, nuts, cinnamon, cardamom and nutmeg; add to creamed mixture until well blended. Stir in "M&M's"® Chocolate Mini Baking Bits. Using 1 tablespoon of dough at a time, form into crescent shapes; place about 2 inches apart onto prepared cookie sheets. Bake 12 to 14 minutes or until edges are golden. Cool 2 minutes on cookie sheets. Gently roll warm crescents in remaining 1 cup sugar. Cool completely on wire racks. Store in tightly covered container.

Makes about 2 dozen cookies

Homemade Coconut Macaroons

- 3 egg whites
- ¼ teaspoon cream of tartar
- ⅛ teaspoon salt
- ¾ cup sugar
- 2¼ cups shredded coconut, toasted*
- 1 teaspoon vanilla

**To toast coconut, spread evenly on ungreased cookie sheet. Toast in preheated 350°F oven 5 to 7 minutes, stirring occasionally until light golden brown.*

1. Preheat oven to 325°F. Line cookie sheets with parchment paper or foil. Beat egg whites, cream of tartar and salt in large bowl with electric mixer until soft peaks form. Beat in sugar, 1 tablespoon at a time, until egg whites are stiff and shiny. Fold in coconut and vanilla. Drop tablespoonfuls of dough 4 inches apart onto prepared cookie sheets; spread each into 3-inch circles with back of spoon.

2. Bake 18 to 22 minutes or until golden brown. Cool 1 minute on cookie sheets. Remove to wire racks; cool completely. Store in airtight container.

Makes about 2 dozen cookies

Spicy Lemon Crescents

Chocolate-Pecan Angels

1 cup mini semisweet chocolate chips
1 cup chopped pecans, toasted
1 cup sifted powdered sugar
1 egg white

1. Preheat oven to 350°F. Grease cookie sheets. Combine chocolate chips, pecans and powdered sugar in medium bowl. Add egg white; mix well. Drop by teaspoonfuls 2 inches apart onto prepared cookie sheets.

2. Bake 11 to 12 minutes or until edges are light golden brown. Let cookies stand on cookie sheets 1 minute. Remove cookies to wire racks; cool completely. *Makes about 3 dozen cookies*

Peanut Butter & Banana Cookies

¼ cup (½ stick) butter
½ cup mashed ripe banana
½ cup no-sugar-added natural peanut butter
¼ cup thawed frozen unsweetened apple juice concentrate
1 egg
1 teaspoon vanilla
1 cup all-purpose flour
½ teaspoon baking soda
¼ teaspoon salt
½ cup chopped salted peanuts
Whole salted peanuts (optional)

Preheat oven to 375°F. Grease cookie sheets. Beat butter in large bowl until creamy. Add banana and peanut butter; beat until smooth. Blend in apple juice concentrate, egg and vanilla. Beat in flour, baking soda and salt. Stir in chopped peanuts. Drop rounded tablespoonfuls of dough 2 inches apart onto prepared cookie sheets; top each with one whole peanut, if desired. Bake 8 minutes or until set. Cool completely on wire racks. Store in tightly covered container. *Makes 2 dozen cookies*

Chocolate-Pecan Angels

Walnut-Orange Chocolate Chippers

1½ cups all-purpose flour
½ cup packed brown sugar
½ cup granulated sugar
1½ teaspoons baking powder
½ teaspoon salt
⅓ cup butter, softened
2 eggs, slightly beaten
2 cups (12 ounces) semisweet chocolate chips
1 cup coarsely chopped California walnuts
2 tablespoons grated orange rind

Combine flour, brown sugar, granulated sugar, baking powder and salt in large bowl; mix in butter and eggs. Add remaining ingredients and mix thoroughly (batter will be stiff). Drop tablespoonfuls of dough 2 inches apart onto ungreased cookies sheets. Bake in preheated 350°F oven 9 to 11 minutes or until lightly browned. Cool 1 minute on cookie sheets; transfer to wire racks to cool completely.

Makes about 3½ dozen cookies

Variation: Prepare dough as directed above. Spread evenly into greased and floured 9-inch square pan (use wet hands to smooth). Bake at 350°F 25 minutes or until golden brown. Cool; cut into 36 squares.

Favorite recipe from **Walnut Marketing Board**

Fudgy Oatmeal Butterscotch Cookies

1 package (18.25 ounces) devil's food cake mix
1½ cups quick-cooking or old-fashioned oats, uncooked
¾ cup (1½ sticks) butter, melted
2 large eggs
1 tablespoon vegetable oil
1 teaspoon vanilla extract
1¼ cups "M&M's"® Chocolate Mini Baking Bits
1 cup butterscotch chips

Preheat oven to 350°F. In large bowl combine cake mix, oats, butter, eggs, oil and vanilla until well blended. Stir in "M&M's"® Chocolate Mini Baking Bits and butterscotch chips. Drop by heaping tablespoonfuls about 2 inches apart onto ungreased cookie sheets. Bake 10 to 12 minutes. Cool 1 minute on cookie sheets; cool completely on wire racks. Store in tightly covered container. *Makes about 3 dozen cookies*

Walnut-Orange Chocolate Chippers

Chocolate Peanut Butter Cookies

- 1 package DUNCAN HINES® Moist Deluxe® Devil's Food Cake Mix
- ¾ cup crunchy peanut butter
- 2 eggs
- 2 tablespoons milk
- 1 cup candy-coated peanut butter pieces

1. Preheat oven to 350°F. Grease baking sheets.

2. Combine cake mix, peanut butter, eggs and milk in large mixing bowl. Beat at low speed with electric mixer until blended. Stir in peanut butter pieces.

3. Drop dough by slightly rounded tablespoonfuls onto prepared baking sheets. Bake 7 to 9 minutes or until lightly browned. Cool 2 minutes on baking sheets. Remove to cooling racks. Cool completely. Store in airtight container.

Makes about 3½ dozen cookies

Tip: You can use 1 cup peanut butter chips in place of peanut butter pieces.

Orange Pecan Gems

- 1 package DUNCAN HINES® Moist Deluxe® Orange Supreme Cake Mix
- 1 container (8 ounces) vanilla low fat yogurt
- 1 egg
- 2 tablespoons butter or margarine, softened
- 1 cup finely chopped pecans
- 1 cup pecan halves

1. Preheat oven to 350°F. Grease baking sheets.

2. Combine cake mix, yogurt, egg, butter and chopped pecans in large bowl. Beat at low speed with electric mixer until blended.

3. Drop by rounded teaspoonfuls 2 inches apart onto prepared baking sheets. Press pecan half into center of each cookie. Bake 11 to 13 minutes or until golden brown. Cool 1 minute on baking sheets. Remove to cooling racks. Cool completely. Store in airtight container.

Makes 4½ to 5 dozen cookies

Quick Tip

Yogurt is a creamy, somewhat tart cultured dairy product made by fermenting whole, low-fat or skim milk with a bacterial culture. It has been a staple in the Middle East and Eastern Europe for centuries, but it was not commercially available in the United States until 1940 and did not become popular until the 1970's. Yogurt is available plain, flavored and frozen.

Chocolate Peanut Butter Cookies

Lemon Melts

½ cup canola oil
½ cup (1 stick) butter, melted
½ cup packed brown sugar
½ cup powdered sugar
1 tablespoon lemon juice
1 tablespoon vanilla
1½ teaspoons almond extract
2 cups all-purpose flour
½ teaspoon cream of tartar
½ teaspoon baking soda

1. Preheat oven to 350°F. Grease cookie sheets.

2. Beat oil, butter, sugars, lemon juice, vanilla and almond extract in large bowl with electric mixer at medium speed until creamy.

3. Combine flour, cream of tartar and baking soda in separate bowl. Gradually beat into butter mixture until stiff dough forms.

4. Drop dough by rounded tablespoonfuls 2 inches apart onto prepared cookie sheets; flatten gently with fork. Bake 20 minutes or until cookies brown around edges only. Cool cookies on cookie sheets 1 minute. Remove to wire racks; cool completely. *Makes about 40 cookies*

Quick and Easy Jumbles

1 package (about 17 ounces) sugar cookie mix
½ cup (1 stick) butter, melted
1 egg, lightly beaten
½ cup mini candy-coated chocolate pieces or ½ cup semisweet chocolate chips
½ cup raisins
½ cup coarsely chopped walnuts

1. Preheat oven to 350°F.

2. Combine cookie mix, butter and egg in large bowl. Stir with spoon until well blended. Stir in chocolate pieces, raisins and walnuts.

3. Drop dough by rounded teaspoonfuls onto *ungreased* cookie sheets about 2 inches apart. Bake for 7 to 8 minutes or until set. Cool 1 minute on cookie sheets. Remove cookies to wire racks; cool completely.

Makes about 2 dozen cookies

Lemon Melts

Chocolate Macadamia Chippers

1 package (18 ounces) refrigerated chocolate chip cookie dough
3 tablespoons unsweetened cocoa powder
½ cup coarsely chopped macadamia nuts
Powdered sugar (optional)

1. Preheat oven to 375°F. Remove dough from wrapper; let stand at room temperature about 15 minutes.

2. Place dough in medium bowl; stir in cocoa until well blended. (Dough may be kneaded lightly, if desired.) Stir in nuts. Drop by heaping tablespoons 2 inches apart onto ungreased cookie sheets.

3. Bake 9 to 11 minutes or until almost set. Transfer to wire racks to cool completely. Dust lightly with powdered sugar, if desired.

Makes 2 dozen cookies

Quick Tip

Macadamia nuts are small, round nuts that have hard brown shells with cream colored meat and a buttery rich, slightly sweet flavor. Most are sold shelled, either roasted or raw. They are the world's most expensive nut and considered by many to also be the world's finest.

Oatmeal Cookies

1 cup all-purpose flour
1 teaspoon baking powder
½ teaspoon baking soda
½ teaspoon salt
¼ cup MOTT'S® Cinnamon Apple Sauce
2 tablespoons margarine
½ cup granulated sugar
½ cup firmly packed light brown sugar
1 egg or ¼ cup egg substitute
1 teaspoon vanilla extract
1⅓ cups uncooked rolled oats
½ cup raisins (optional)

Heat oven to 375°F. Lightly spray cookie sheet with cooking spray. In large bowl, mix flour, baking powder, baking soda and salt. In separate bowl, beat together apple sauce, margarine, granulated and brown sugars, egg and vanilla until margarine forms pea-sized pieces. Add flour mixture to apple sauce mixture. Mix well. Fold in oats and raisins. Drop rounded teaspoonfuls dough onto cookie sheet; bake 5 minutes. Remove cookies from cookie sheet and cool completely on wire rack.

Makes 36 cookies

Chocolate Macadamia Chippers

Bars & Brownies

Chocolate Nut Bars

1¾ cups graham cracker crumbs
½ cup (1 stick) butter or margarine, melted
1 (14-ounce) can EAGLE BRAND® Sweetened Condensed Milk (NOT evaporated milk)
2 cups (12 ounces) semi-sweet chocolate chips, divided
1 teaspoon vanilla extract
1 cup chopped nuts

1. Preheat oven to 375°F. In medium mixing bowl, combine crumbs and butter; press firmly on bottom of ungreased 13×9-inch baking pan. Bake 8 minutes. Reduce oven temperature to 350°F.

2. In small saucepan, melt EAGLE BRAND® with 1 cup chips and vanilla. Spread chocolate mixture over prepared crust. Top with remaining 1 cup chips and nuts; press down firmly.

3. Bake 25 to 30 minutes. Cool. Chill, if desired. Cut into bars. Store loosely covered at room temperature.

Makes 2 to 3 dozen bars

Prep Time: 10 minutes
Bake Time: 33 to 38 minutes

Chocolate Nut Bars

Yuletide Linzer Bars

1⅓ cups butter, softened
¾ cup sugar
1 egg
1 teaspoon grated lemon peel
2½ cups all-purpose flour
1½ cups whole almonds, ground
1 teaspoon ground cinnamon
¾ cup raspberry preserves
Powdered sugar

1. Preheat oven to 350°F. Grease 13×9-inch baking pan.

2. Beat butter and sugar in large bowl at medium speed of electric mixer until creamy. Beat in egg and lemon peel until blended. Mix in flour, almonds and cinnamon until well blended.

3. Press 2 cups dough onto bottom of prepared pan. Spread preserves over crust. Press remaining dough, a small amount at a time, evenly over preserves.

4. Bake 35 to 40 minutes until golden brown. Cool in pan on wire rack. Sprinkle with powdered sugar; cut into bars. *Makes 36 bars*

Apricot Bars

2 eggs
1 cup no-sugar-added apricot fruit spread
½ cup (1 stick) butter, melted
2 teaspoons vanilla
1 cup all-purpose flour
⅔ cup uncooked old-fashioned oats
1¼ teaspoons baking powder
¾ teaspoon ground cinnamon
¼ teaspoon salt
¼ teaspoon allspice
⅛ teaspoon mace

Preheat oven to 350°F. Beat eggs in large bowl. Blend in fruit spread, butter and vanilla. Add flour, oats, baking powder, cinnamon, salt, allspice and mace; mix well. Spread dough into greased 12×8-inch baking dish. Bake 18 minutes or until golden brown and firm to the touch. Cool completely on wire rack. Cut into bars. Store in tightly covered container. *Makes 1½ dozen bars*

Quick Tip

Mace is a spice made of the red membranes covering nutmeg seeds. The color becomes yellow-orange after being removed from the seeds and dried. It tastes and smells a lot like nutmeg, but has a much stronger flavor. Most often it is ground, but occasionally you may find it whole.

Yuletide Linzer Bars

Cheesecake-Topped Brownies

1 (21.5- or 23.6-ounce) package fudge brownie mix
1 (8-ounce) package cream cheese, softened
2 tablespoons butter or margarine, softened
1 tablespoon cornstarch
1 (14-ounce) can EAGLE BRAND® Sweetened Condensed Milk (NOT evaporated milk)
1 egg
2 teaspoons vanilla extract
Ready-to-spread chocolate frosting, if desired
Orange peel, if desired

1. Preheat oven to 350°F. Prepare brownie mix as package directs. Spread into well-greased 13×9-inch baking pan.

2. In large mixing bowl, beat cream cheese, butter and cornstarch until fluffy.

3. Gradually beat in EAGLE BRAND®. Add egg and vanilla; beat until smooth. Pour cheesecake mixture evenly over brownie batter.

4. Bake 40 to 45 minutes or until top is lightly browned. Cool. Spread with frosting or sprinkle with orange peel, if desired. Cut into bars. Store covered in refrigerator.

Makes 3 to 3½ dozen brownies

Prep Time: 20 minutes
Bake Time: 40 to 45 minutes

Oatmeal Toffee Bars

1 cup (2 sticks) butter or margarine, softened
1 cup packed light brown sugar
2 eggs
1 teaspoon vanilla extract
1½ cups all-purpose flour
1 teaspoon baking soda
½ teaspoon ground cinnamon
½ teaspoon salt
1⅓ cups (8-ounce package) HEATH® BITS 'O BRICKLE® Toffee Bits, divided
3 cups quick-cooking or regular rolled oats

1. Heat oven to 350°F. Grease 13×9×2-inch baking pan.

2. Beat butter and brown sugar in large bowl until well blended. Add eggs and vanilla; beat well. Stir together flour, baking soda, cinnamon and salt; gradually add to butter mixture, beating until well blended. Set aside ¼ cup toffee bits. Stir remaining toffee bits and oats into batter (batter will be stiff). Spread batter in prepared pan; sprinkle reserved ¼ cup toffee bits over surface.

3. Bake 25 minutes or until wooden pick inserted in center comes out clean. Cool completely in pan on wire rack. Cut into bars.

Makes about 36 bars

Cheesecake-Topped Brownies

Holiday Red Raspberry Chocolate Bars

2½ cups all-purpose flour
1 cup sugar
¾ cup finely chopped pecans
1 egg, beaten
1 cup (2 sticks) cold butter or margarine
1 jar (12 ounces) seedless red raspberry jam
1⅔ cups HERSHEY'S Milk Chocolate Chips, HERSHEY'S Semi-Sweet Chocolate Chips, HERSHEY'S Raspberry Chips or HERSHEY'S MINI KISSES® Milk Chocolates

1. Heat oven to 350°F. Grease 13×9×2-inch baking pan.

2. Stir together flour, sugar, pecans and egg in large bowl. Cut in butter with pastry blender or fork until mixture resembles coarse crumbs; set aside 1½ cups crumb mixture. Press remaining crumb mixture on bottom of prepared pan. Stir jam to soften; carefully spread over crumb mixture. Sprinkle with chocolate chips. Crumble remaining crumb mixture evenly over top.

3. Bake 40 to 45 minutes or until lightly browned. Cool completely in pan on wire rack; cut into bars. *Makes 36 bars*

Peanut Butter Shortbreads

½ cup (1 stick) unsalted butter, softened
½ cup granulated sugar
¼ cup creamy peanut butter
2 cups all-purpose flour

Preheat oven to 300°F. In bowl, combine all ingredients with your fingers until mixture resembles coarse meal. Press the mixture into an ungreased 8-inch round baking pan. With a fork, prick decorative wedges in the dough. Bake for about 1 hour or until very lightly browned. Cut into wedges while warm.

Makes 16 wedge-shaped cookies

Favorite recipe from **Peanut Advisory Board**

Toffee Bars

½ cup (1 stick) butter, softened
½ cup packed light brown sugar
1 egg yolk
1 teaspoon vanilla
1 cup all-purpose flour
1 cup (6 ounces) milk chocolate chips
½ cup chopped walnuts or pecans

Preheat oven to 350°F. Lightly grease 13×9-inch pan. Cream butter and sugar in large bowl. Blend in egg yolk and vanilla. Stir in flour until well blended. Press on bottom of prepared pan. Bake 15 minutes or until golden. Remove from oven; sprinkle chocolate chips over top. Let stand a few minutes until chips melt, then spread evenly over bars. Sprinkle nuts over chocolate. Score into 2×1½-inch bars while still warm. Cool completely in pan on wire rack before cutting and removing from pan. *Makes about 3 dozen bars*

Holiday Red Raspberry Chocolate Bars

Lemon-Cranberry Bars

½ cup frozen lemonade concentrate, thawed
½ cup sugar substitute
¼ cup (½ stick) margarine, softened
1 egg
1½ cups all-purpose flour
2 teaspoons grated lemon peel
½ teaspoon baking soda
½ teaspoon salt
½ cup dried cranberries

1. Preheat oven to 375°F. Lightly coat 8-inch square baking pan with nonstick cooking spray; set aside.

2. Combine lemonade concentrate, sugar substitute, margarine and egg in medium bowl; mix well. Add flour, lemon peel, baking soda and salt; stir well. Stir in cranberries; spoon into prepared pan.

3. Bake 20 minutes or until light brown. Cool completely in pan on wire rack. Cut into 16 squares.

Makes 16 bars

Seven-Layer Dessert

½ cup (1 stick) butter, melted
1 teaspoon vanilla
1 cup graham cracker crumbs
1 cup butterscotch chips
1 cup chocolate chips
1 cup shredded coconut
1 cup nuts
1 can (14 ounces) sweetened condensed milk

Preheat oven to 350°F. Pour butter into 13×9-inch baking dish. Add vanilla. Sprinkle cracker crumbs over butter. Layer butterscotch chips over crumbs, followed by chocolate chips, coconut and nuts. Pour milk over mixture. Bake 25 minutes or until lightly browned.

Makes 12 to 18 bars

Quick Tip

Sweetened condensed milk is a canned product that is the result of evaporating about half of the water from whole milk and adding cane sugar or corn syrup to sweeten and preserve the milk. The thick sweetened milk is used for desserts and candy. It should not be confused with evaporated milk.

Lemon-Cranberry Bars

Hershey®s Best Brownies

1 cup (2 sticks) butter or margarine
2 cups sugar
2 teaspoons vanilla extract
4 eggs
¾ cup HERSHEY®S Cocoa or HERSHEY®S Dutch Processed Cocoa
1 cup all-purpose flour
½ teaspoon baking powder
¼ teaspoon salt
1 cup chopped nuts (optional)

1. Heat oven to 350°F. Grease 13×9×2-inch baking pan.

2. Place butter in large microwave-safe bowl. Microwave at HIGH (100% power) 2 to 2½ minutes or until melted. Stir in sugar and vanilla. Add eggs, one at a time, beating well with spoon after each addition. Add cocoa; beat until well blended. Add flour, baking powder and salt; beat well. Stir in nuts, if desired. Pour batter into prepared pan.

3. Bake 30 to 35 minutes or until brownies begin to pull away from sides of pan. Cool completely in pan on wire rack. Cut into bars.

Makes about 36 brownies

Butterscotch Bars

¾ cup all-purpose flour
½ cup packed brown sugar
½ cup fat-free butterscotch ice cream topping
¼ cup cholesterol-free egg substitute
3 tablespoons margarine or butter, melted
1 teaspoon vanilla
¼ teaspoon salt
½ cup toasted chopped pecans (optional)

1. Preheat oven to 350°F. Lightly coat 8-inch square baking pan with nonstick cooking spray; set aside.

2. Combine all ingredients in medium bowl; stir until blended. Spread into prepared pan.

3. Bake 15 to 18 minutes or until firm to touch. Cool completely in pan. Cut into 16 bars.

Makes 16 servings

Tip: These sweet bars are the perfect packable treat. Wrap individually in plastic wrap so they will be ready to grab for the lunch box or a spur-of-the-moment picnic in the park.

Pumpkin Harvest Bars

1¾ cups all-purpose flour
2 teaspoons baking powder
1 teaspoon grated orange peel
1 teaspoon ground cinnamon
½ teaspoon salt
½ teaspoon ground nutmeg
¼ teaspoon ground ginger
¼ teaspoon ground cloves
¾ cup sugar
½ cup MOTT'S® Natural Apple Sauce
½ cup solid-pack pumpkin
1 whole egg
1 egg white
2 tablespoons vegetable oil
½ cup raisins

1. Preheat oven to 350°F. Spray 13×9-inch baking pan with nonstick cooking spray.

2. In small bowl, combine flour, baking powder, orange peel, cinnamon, salt, nutmeg, ginger and cloves.

3. In large bowl, combine sugar, apple sauce, pumpkin, whole egg, egg white and oil.

4. Add flour mixture to apple sauce mixture; stir until well blended. Stir in raisins. Spread batter into prepared pan.

5. Bake 25 to 30 minutes or until toothpick inserted in center comes out clean. Cool on wire rack 15 minutes; cut into 16 bars.

Makes 16 servings

Toffee Diamonds

1 cup (2 sticks) I CAN'T BELIEVE IT'S NOT BUTTER!® Spread, softened
2 cups all-purpose flour
1 cup firmly packed brown sugar
1 egg, separated
½ teaspoon vanilla extract
1 cup chopped walnuts

Preheat oven to 325°F. Grease 15½×10½-inch jelly-roll pan; set aside.

In large bowl, with electric mixer, beat I Can't Believe It's Not Butter!® Spread, flour, sugar, egg yolk and vanilla until well blended. Evenly spread dough into prepared pan. With fork, beat egg white slightly. With pastry brush, brush egg white over top of flour mixture; sprinkle with walnuts.

Bake 30 minutes or until golden. Remove from oven and immediately cut into diamonds. Remove from pan to wire rack; cool completely.

Makes 4 dozen diamonds

Quick Tip

Jelly-roll pans are rectangular baking pans with 1-inch-high sides and are usually used to make thin sponge cakes that can be spread with jelly and rolled. These pans can also be used for making bar cookies or thin sheet cakes. A standard pan measures 15½×10½×1-inch. They are available in aluminum and steel.

Pumpkin Harvest Bars

Cindy's Fudgy Brownies

1 (21-ounce) package DUNCAN HINES® Family-Style Chewy Fudge Brownie Mix
1 egg
⅓ cup water
⅓ cup vegetable oil
¾ cup semisweet chocolate chips
½ cup chopped pecans

1. Preheat oven to 350°F. Grease bottom only of 13×9×2-inch pan.

2. Combine brownie mix, egg, water and oil in large bowl. Stir with spoon until well blended, about 50 strokes. Stir in chocolate chips. Spread in prepared pan. Sprinkle with pecans. Bake at 350°F for 25 to 28 minutes or until set. Cool completely. Cut into bars. *Makes 24 brownies*

Tip: Overbaking brownies will cause them to become dry. Follow the recommended baking times given in recipes closely.

Pineapple Almond Shortbread Bars

Crust

1½ cups all-purpose flour
½ cup almonds, toasted, ground
¼ cup sugar
½ cup (1 stick) cold margarine

Topping

1 can (20 ounces) DOLE® Crushed Pineapple, drained
3 eggs
¼ cup honey
¼ cup sugar
1 tablespoon grated lemon peel
1½ cups slivered almonds, toasted

For Crust, preheat oven to 350°F. In large bowl, combine flour, almonds and sugar. Cut in margarine until crumbly. Form dough into a ball; press into ungreased 13×9-inch baking pan. Bake 10 minutes. Cool slightly.

For Topping, in medium bowl, combine crushed pineapple, eggs, honey, sugar and lemon peel. Stir in almonds. Pour topping over partially baked crust. Bake an additional 30 to 35 minutes. Cool completely in pan on wire rack. Cut into bars. *Makes about 2 dozen bars*

Cindy's Fudgy Brownies

Peanut Butter Chips and Jelly Bars

1½ cups all-purpose flour
½ cup sugar
¾ teaspoon baking powder
½ cup (1 stick) cold butter or margarine
1 egg, beaten
¾ cup grape jelly
1⅔ cups (10-ounce package) REESE'S® Peanut Butter Chips, divided

1. Heat oven to 375°F. Grease 9-inch square baking pan.

2. Stir together flour, sugar and baking powder in large bowl. With pastry blender or two knives, cut in butter until mixture resembles coarse crumbs. Add egg; blend well. Reserve 1 cup mixture; press remaining mixture onto bottom of prepared pan. Stir jelly to soften; spread evenly over crust. Sprinkle 1 cup peanut butter chips over jelly. Stir together reserved crumb mixture with remaining ⅔ cup chips; sprinkle over top.

3. Bake 25 to 30 minutes or until lightly browned. Cool completely in pan on wire rack. Cut into bars.

Makes about 16 bars

Coconut Butterscotch Bars

½ cup (1 stick) butter or margarine, softened
½ cup powdered sugar
1 cup all-purpose flour
1 can (14 ounces) sweetened condensed milk (not evaporated milk)
1 cup HERSHEY'S Butterscotch Chips
1⅓ cups MOUNDS® Sweetened Coconut Flakes
1 teaspoon vanilla extract

1. Heat oven to 350°F.

2. Beat butter and powdered sugar in bowl until blended. Add flour; mix well. Pat mixture onto bottom of ungreased 9-inch square baking pan. Bake 12 to 15 minutes or until lightly browned. Combine sweetened condensed milk, butterscotch chips, coconut and vanilla; spread over baked layer.

3. Bake 25 to 30 minutes or until golden brown around edges. (Center will not appear set.) Cool completely in pan on wire rack. Cut into bars.

Makes 36 bars

Quick Tip

Brownies and bars make great gifts! Place them in a paper-lined tin or on a decorative plate; cover with plastic wrap and tie with a colorful ribbon. For a special touch, you can include the recipe.

Peanut Butter Chips and Jelly Bars

Quick & Easy Fudgey Brownies

- 4 bars (1 ounce each) HERSHEY®S Unsweetened Baking Chocolate, broken into pieces
- ¾ cup (1½ sticks) butter or margarine
- 2 cups sugar
- 3 eggs
- 1½ teaspoons vanilla extract
- 1 cup all-purpose flour
- 1 cup chopped nuts (optional)
- Creamy Quick Chocolate Frosting (recipe follows, optional)

1. Heat oven to 350°F. Grease 13×9×2-inch baking pan.

2. Place chocolate and butter in large microwave-safe bowl. Microwave at HIGH (100%) 1½ to 2 minutes or until chocolate is melted and mixture is smooth when stirred. Add sugar; stir with spoon until well blended. Add eggs and vanilla; mix well. Add flour and nuts, if desired; stir until well blended. Spread into prepared pan.

3. Bake 30 to 35 minutes or until wooden pick inserted in center comes out almost clean. Cool in pan on wire rack. Frost with Creamy Quick Chocolate Frosting, if desired. Cut into squares.

Makes about 24 brownies

Creamy Quick Chocolate Frosting: Place 3 tablespoons butter and 3 bars (1 ounce each) Hershey®s Unsweetened Baking Chocolate, broken into pieces, in saucepan over very low heat. Heat, stirring constantly, until chocolate is melted and mixture is smooth. Pour into large bowl; add 3 cups powdered sugar, ½ cup milk, 1 teaspoon vanilla extract and ⅛ teaspoon salt. Beat on medium speed of mixer until well blended. If necessary, refrigerate 10 minutes or until of spreading consistency. Makes about 2 cups frosting.

Buckeye Cookie Bars

- 1 (18¼-ounce) package chocolate cake mix
- ¼ cup vegetable oil
- 1 egg
- 1 cup chopped peanuts
- 1 (14-ounce) can EAGLE BRAND® Sweetened Condensed Milk (NOT evaporated milk)
- ½ cup peanut butter

1. Preheat oven to 350°F. In large mixing bowl, combine cake mix, oil and egg; beat at medium speed of electric mixer until crumbly. Stir in peanuts. Reserve 1½ cups crumb mixture; press remaining crumb mixture firmly on bottom of greased 13×9-inch baking pan.

2. In medium mixing bowl, beat EAGLE BRAND® with peanut butter until smooth; spread over prepared crust. Sprinkle with reserved crumb mixture.

3. Bake 25 to 30 minutes or until set. Cool. Cut into bars. Store loosely covered at room temperature. *Makes 24 to 36 bars*

Prep Time: 20 minutes
Bake Time: 25 to 30 minutes

Quick & Easy Fudgey Brownies

Fruit and Oat Squares

- 1 cup all-purpose flour
- 1 cup uncooked quick oats
- ¾ cup packed light brown sugar
- ½ teaspoon baking soda
- ¼ teaspoon salt
- ¼ teaspoon ground cinnamon
- ⅓ cup butter or margarine, melted
- ¾ cup apricot, cherry or other fruit flavor preserves

1. Preheat oven to 350°F. Spray 9-inch square baking pan with nonstick cooking spray; set aside.

2. Combine flour, oats, brown sugar, baking soda, salt and cinnamon in medium bowl; mix well. Add butter; stir with fork until mixture is crumbly. Reserve ¾ cup crumb mixture for topping. Press remaining crumb mixture evenly onto bottom of prepared pan. Bake 5 to 7 minutes or until lightly browned. Spread preserves over crust; sprinkle with reserved crumb mixture.

3. Bake 20 to 25 minutes or until golden brown. Cool completely in pan on wire rack. Cut into 16 squares. *Makes 16 servings*

Tip: Store individually wrapped Fruit and Oat Squares at room temperature up to 3 days or freeze up to 1 month.

Strawberry Streusel Bars

Crumb Mixture

- 2 cups all-purpose flour
- 1 cup sugar
- ¾ cup pecans, coarsely chopped
- 1 cup (2 sticks) butter, softened
- 1 egg

Filling

- 1 jar (10 ounces) strawberry preserves

1. Preheat oven to 350°F. Grease 9-inch square baking pan. Set aside.

2. For crumb mixture, combine flour, sugar, pecans, butter and egg in large mixer bowl. Beat at low speed of electric mixer, scraping bowl often, until mixture is crumbly, 2 to 3 minutes. Reserve 1 cup crumb mixture; press remaining crumb mixture onto bottom of prepared baking pan. Spread preserves to within ½ inch of edges. Crumble remaining crumb mixture over preserves. Bake 42 to 50 minutes or until lightly browned. Cool completely. Cut into bars.

Makes about 24 bars

Fruit and Oat Squares

Hershey®s White Chip Brownies

4 eggs
1¼ cups sugar
½ cup (1 stick) butter or margarine, melted
2 teaspoons vanilla extract
1⅓ cups all-purpose flour
⅔ cup HERSHEY®S Cocoa
1 teaspoon baking powder
½ teaspoon salt
2 cups (12-ounce package) HERSHEY®S Premier White Chips

1. Heat oven to 350°F. Grease 13×9×2-inch baking pan.

2. Beat eggs in large bowl until foamy; gradually beat in sugar. Add butter and vanilla; beat until blended. Stir together flour, cocoa, baking powder and salt; add to egg mixture, beating until blended. Stir in white chips. Spread batter into prepared pan.

3. Bake 25 to 30 minutes or until brownies begin to pull away from sides of pan. Cool completely in pan on wire rack. Cut into squares.

Makes about 36 brownies

Tip: Brownies and bar cookies cut into different shapes can add interest to a plate of simple square cookies. Cut cookies into different size rectangles or make triangles by cutting them into 2- to 2½-inch squares; cut each square in half diagonally. To make diamond shapes, cut straight lines 1 or 1½ inches apart the length of the baking pan, then cut straight lines 1½ inches apart diagonally across the pan.

Prep Time: 15 minutes
Bake Time: 25 minutes
Cool Time: 2 hours

Peachy Oatmeal Bars

Crumb Mixture

1½ cups all-purpose flour
1 cup uncooked old-fashioned oats
¾ cup (1½ sticks) butter, melted
½ cup sugar
2 teaspoons almond extract
½ teaspoon baking soda
¼ teaspoon salt

Filling

¾ cup peach preserves
⅓ cup flaked coconut

1. Preheat oven to 350°F. Grease 9-inch square baking pan.

2. Combine flour, oats, butter, sugar, almond extract, baking soda and salt in large bowl. Beat with electric mixer at low speed 1 to 2 minutes until mixture is crumbly. Reserve ¾ cup crumb mixture; press remaining crumb mixture onto bottom of prepared baking pan.

3. Spread peach preserves to within ½ inch of edge of crumb mixture; sprinkle reserved crumb mixture and coconut over top. Bake 22 to 27 minutes or until edges are lightly browned. Cool completely. Cut into bars.

Makes 2 to 2½ dozen bars

Hershey's White Chip Brownies

Apricot Crumb Squares

1 package (18¼ ounces) light yellow cake mix
1 teaspoon ground cinnamon
½ teaspoon ground nutmeg
¼ cup plus 2 tablespoons cold margarine, cut into pieces
¾ cup uncooked multigrain oatmeal cereal or old-fashioned oats
1 whole egg
2 egg whites
1 tablespoon water
1 jar (10 ounces) apricot fruit spread
2 tablespoons packed light brown sugar

1. Preheat oven to 350°F. Combine cake mix, cinnamon and nutmeg in medium bowl. Cut in margarine with pastry blender or 2 knives until coarse crumbs form. Stir in cereal. Reserve 1 cup crumb mixture. Add egg, egg whites and water to remaining crumb mixture; stir until well blended.

2. Spread evenly in ungreased 13×9-inch baking pan; top with fruit spread. Sprinkle reserved crumb mixture over fruit spread; sprinkle with brown sugar.

3. Bake 35 to 40 minutes or until top is golden brown. Cool in pan on wire rack; cut into 15 squares. *Makes 15 servings*

Double Chocolate Chewies

1 package DUNCAN HINES® Moist Deluxe® Butter Recipe Fudge Cake Mix
2 eggs
½ cup (1 stick) butter or margarine, melted
1 package (6 ounces) semisweet chocolate chips
1 cup chopped nuts
Confectioners' sugar (optional)

1. Preheat oven to 350°F. Grease bottom only of 13×9×2-inch pan.

2. Combine cake mix, eggs and melted butter in large bowl. Stir until thoroughly blended. (Mixture will be stiff.) Stir in chocolate chips and nuts. Press mixture evenly in prepared pan. Bake at 350°F for 25 to 30 minutes or until toothpick inserted in center comes out clean. *Do not overbake.* Cool completely. Cut into bars. Dust with confectioners' sugar, if desired. *Makes 36 bars*

Quick Tip

For a special effect, cut a paper towel into ¼-inch-wide strips. Place strips in diagonal pattern on top of cooled bars before cutting. Place confectioners' sugar in tea strainer. Tap strainer lightly to dust surface with sugar. Carefully remove strips.

Apricot Crumb Squares

Cupcakes & Muffins

Strawberry Muffins

1¼ cups all-purpose flour
2½ teaspoons baking powder
½ teaspoon salt
1 cup uncooked old-fashioned oats
½ cup sugar
1 cup milk
½ cup (1 stick) butter, melted
1 egg, beaten
1 teaspoon vanilla
1 cup chopped fresh strawberries

1. Preheat oven to 425°F. Grease bottoms only of 12 (2½-inch) muffin cups or line with paper liners; set aside.

2. Combine flour, baking powder and salt in large bowl. Stir in oats and sugar. Combine milk, butter, egg and vanilla in small bowl until well blended; stir into flour mixture just until moistened. Fold in strawberries. Spoon into prepared muffin cups, filling about two-thirds full.

3. Bake 15 to 18 minutes or until lightly browned and toothpick inserted in centers come out clean. Remove from pan. Cool on wire rack 10 minutes. Serve warm or cool completely.

Makes 12 muffins

White Chocolate Chunk Muffins

2½ cups all-purpose flour
1 cup packed light brown sugar
⅓ cup unsweetened cocoa powder
2 teaspoons baking soda
½ teaspoon salt
1⅓ cups buttermilk
¼ cup plus 2 tablespoons butter, melted
2 eggs, beaten
1½ teaspoons vanilla
1½ cups chopped white chocolate

1. Preheat oven to 400°F. Grease 12 jumbo (3½-inch) muffin cups; set aside.

2. Combine flour, sugar, cocoa, baking soda and salt in large bowl. Combine buttermilk, butter, eggs and vanilla in small bowl until blended. Stir into flour mixture just until moistened. Fold in white chocolate. Spoon into prepared muffin cups, filling half full.

3. Bake 25 to 30 minutes or until toothpick inserted into centers come out clean. Cool in pan on wire rack 5 minutes. Remove from pan. Cool on wire rack 10 minutes. Serve warm or cool completely.

Makes 12 large muffins

Broccoli & Cheddar Muffins

3 cups buttermilk baking and pancake mix
2 eggs, lightly beaten
⅔ cup milk
1 teaspoon dried basil
1 cup (4 ounces) shredded Cheddar cheese
1 box (10 ounces) BIRDS EYE® frozen Chopped Broccoli, thawed and drained

• Preheat oven to 350°F. Combine baking mix, eggs, milk and basil. Mix until moistened. (Do not overmix.)

• Add cheese and broccoli; stir just to combine. Add salt and pepper to taste.

• Spray 12 muffin cups with nonstick cooking spray. Pour batter into muffin cups. Bake 25 to 30 minutes or until golden brown.

• Cool 5 minutes in pan. Loosen sides of muffins with knife; remove from pan and serve warm.

Makes 1 dozen large muffins

Southwestern Corn Muffins: Prepare 1 box corn muffin mix according to package directions; add ⅔ cup BIRDS EYE® frozen Corn and 1 teaspoon chili powder to batter. Mix well; bake according to package directions.

Prep Time: 5 to 10 minutes
Bake Time: 25 to 30 minutes

White Chocolate Chunk Muffins

Angel Almond Cupcakes

1 package DUNCAN HINES® Angel Food Cake Mix
1¼ cups water
2 teaspoons almond extract
1 container DUNCAN HINES® Wild Cherry Vanilla Frosting

1. Preheat oven to 350°F.

2. Combine cake mix, water and almond extract in large bowl. Beat at low speed with electric mixer until moistened. Beat at medium speed for 1 minute. Line medium muffin pans with paper baking cups. Fill muffin cups two-thirds full. Bake at 350°F for 20 to 25 minutes or until golden brown, cracked and dry on top. Remove from muffin pans. Cool completely. Frost with frosting.

Makes 30 to 32 cupcakes

To easily fill muffin cups, place butter in a 4-cup measure. Use a spatula to control the flow of the batter.

Ham and Cheese Corn Muffins

1 package (about 8 ounces) corn muffin mix
½ cup chopped deli ham
½ cup (2 ounces) shredded Swiss cheese
⅓ cup reduced-fat (2%) milk
1 egg
1 tablespoon Dijon mustard

1. Preheat oven to 400°F. Line 9 (2¾-inch) muffin cups with paper liners.

2. Combine muffin mix, ham and cheese in medium bowl. Beat milk, egg and mustard in 1-cup glass measure. Stir milk mixture into dry ingredients; mix just until moistened.

3. Fill muffin cups two-thirds full with batter. Bake 18 to 20 minutes or until light golden brown. Remove muffin pan to cooling rack. Let stand 5 minutes. Serve warm.

Makes 9 muffins

Serving Suggestion: For added flavor, serve Ham and Cheese Corn Muffins with honey-flavored butter. To prepare, stir together equal amounts of honey and softened butter.

Prep and Cook Time: 30 minutes

Angel Almond Cupcakes

Cherry Orange Poppy Seed Muffins

2 cups all-purpose flour
¾ cup granulated sugar
1 tablespoon baking powder
1 tablespoon poppy seeds
¼ teaspoon salt
1 cup milk
¼ cup (½ stick) butter, melted
1 egg, lightly beaten
½ cup dried tart cherries
3 tablespoons grated orange peel

Combine flour, sugar, baking powder, poppy seeds and salt in large mixing bowl. Add milk, melted butter and egg, stirring just until dry ingredients are moistened. Gently stir in cherries and orange peel. Fill paper-lined muffin cups three-fourths full.

Bake in preheated 400°F oven 18 to 22 minutes or until wooden pick inserted in center comes out clean. Let cool in pan 5 minutes. Remove from pan and serve warm or let cool completely.

Makes 12 *muffins*

Favorite recipe from **Cherry Marketing Institute**

Triple-Chocolate Cupcakes

1 package (18.25 ounces) chocolate cake mix
1 package (4 ounces) chocolate instant pudding and pie filling mix
1 container (8 ounces) sour cream
4 large eggs
½ cup vegetable oil
½ cup warm water
2 cups (12-ounce package) NESTLÉ® TOLL HOUSE® Semi-Sweet Chocolate Morsels
2 containers (16 ounces *each*) prepared frosting
Assorted candy sprinkles

PREHEAT oven to 350°F. Grease or paper-line 30 muffin cups.

COMBINE cake mix, pudding mix, sour cream, eggs, vegetable oil and water in large mixer bowl; beat on low speed just until blended. Beat on high speed for 2 minutes. Stir in morsels. Pour into prepared muffin cups, filling ⅔ full.

BAKE for 25 to 28 minutes or until wooden pick inserted in center comes out clean. Cool in pans for 10 minutes; remove to wire racks to cool completely. Frost; decorate with candy sprinkles.

Makes 30 *cupcakes*

Cherry Orange Poppy Seed Muffins

Caramel Apple Cupcakes

1 package (about 18 ounces) butter or yellow cake mix, plus ingredients to prepare mix
1 cup chopped dried apples
Caramel Frosting (recipe follows)
Chopped nuts (optional)

1. Preheat oven to 375°F. Line 24 standard (2½-inch) muffin pan cups with paper baking cups.

2. Prepare cake mix according to package directions. Stir in apples. Spoon batter into prepared muffin cups.

3. Bake 15 to 20 minutes or until toothpick inserted into centers come out clean. Cool in pans on wire racks 10 minutes. Remove to racks; cool completely.

4. Prepare Caramel Frosting. Frost cupcakes. Sprinkle cupcakes with nuts, if desired.

Makes 24 cupcakes

Caramel Frosting

3 tablespoons butter
1 cup packed light brown sugar
½ cup evaporated milk
⅛ teaspoon salt
3¾ cups powdered sugar
¾ teaspoon vanilla

1. Melt butter in 2-quart saucepan. Stir in brown sugar, evaporated milk and salt. Bring to a boil, stirring constantly. Remove from heat; cool to lukewarm.

2. Add powdered sugar; beat until frosting is of spreading consistency. Add vanilla; beat until smooth.

Southern Biscuit Muffins

2½ cups all-purpose flour
¼ cup sugar
1½ tablespoons baking powder
¾ cup (1½ sticks) cold butter
1 cup cold milk

1. Preheat oven to 400°F. Grease 12 standard (2½-inch) muffin pan cups. (These muffins brown better on the sides and bottoms when baked without paper liners.)

2. Combine flour, sugar and baking powder in large bowl. Cut in butter with pastry blender until mixture resembles coarse crumbs. Stir in milk just until flour mixture is moistened. Spoon evenly into prepared muffin cups.

3. Bake 20 minutes or until golden. Remove from pan. Cool on wire rack. *Makes 12 muffins*

Tip: These muffins taste like baking powder biscuits and are very quick and easy to make. Serve them with jelly, jam or honey.

Caramel Apple Cupcakes

Cinnamon Spiced Muffins

1½ cups all-purpose flour
¾ cup sugar, divided
2 teaspoons baking powder
½ teaspoon salt
½ teaspoon ground nutmeg
½ teaspoon ground coriander
½ teaspoon ground allspice
½ cup milk
⅓ cup butter, melted
1 egg
1 teaspoon ground cinnamon
¼ cup (½ stick) butter, melted

1. Preheat oven to 400°F. Grease 36 (1¾-inch) mini-muffin cups.

2. Combine flour, ½ cup sugar, baking powder, salt, nutmeg, coriander and allspice in large bowl. Combine milk, ⅓ cup butter and egg in small bowl; stir into flour mixture just until moistened. Spoon evenly into prepared muffin cups.

3. Bake 10 to 13 minutes or until edges are lightly browned and toothpick inserted in centers comes out clean. Remove from pan.

4. Meanwhile, combine remaining ¼ cup sugar and cinnamon in shallow dish. Dip warm muffin tops in ¼ cup melted butter, then in sugar-cinnamon mixture. Serve warm.

Makes 36 mini muffins

Apple Streusel Mini Muffins

¼ cup chopped pecans
2 tablespoons brown sugar
1 tablespoon all-purpose flour
2 teaspoons butter, melted
1 package (7 ounces) apple-cinnamon muffin mix
½ cup shredded peeled apple

1. Preheat oven to 425°F. Coat 18 mini-muffin cups with nonstick cooking spray.

2. Combine pecans, brown sugar, flour and butter in small bowl.

3. Prepare muffin mix according to package directions. Stir in apple. Fill each muffin cup ⅔ full. Sprinkle approximately 1 teaspoon pecan mixture on top of each muffin. Bake 12 to 15 minutes or until golden brown. Cool slightly. Serve warm. *Makes 18 mini muffins*

Variation: For regular-size muffins, grease six 2½-inch muffin cups. Prepare topping and batter as directed. Fill muffin cups ⅔ full. Sprinkle approximately 1 tablespoon pecan mixture on each muffin. Bake 18 to 20 minutes or until golden brown. Makes 6 regular muffins.

Prep and Cook Time: 30 minutes

Cinnamon Spiced Muffins

Pretty-in-Pink Peppermint Cupcakes

1 package (about 18 ounces) white cake mix
1⅓ cups water
3 egg whites
2 tablespoons vegetable oil or melted butter
½ teaspoon peppermint extract
3 to 4 drops red liquid food coloring *or* ¼ teaspoon gel food coloring
1 container (16 ounces) prepared vanilla frosting
½ cup crushed peppermint candies (about 16 candies)

1. Preheat oven to 350°F. Line 30 standard (2½-inch) muffin pan cups with pink or white paper baking cups.

2. Beat cake mix, water, egg whites, oil, peppermint extract and food coloring with electric mixer at low speed 30 seconds. Beat at medium speed 2 minutes.

3. Spoon batter into prepared muffin cups filling ¾ full. Bake 20 to 22 minutes or until toothpick inserted into centers come out clean. Cool in pans on wire racks 10 minutes. Remove cupcakes to racks; cool completely. (At this point, cupcakes may be frozen up to 3 months. Thaw at room temperature before frosting.)

4. Spread cooled cupcakes with frosting; sprinkle with crushed candies. Store at room temperature up to 24 hours or cover and refrigerate up to 3 days before serving. *Makes about 30 cupcakes*

Coconut Cupcakes

1 package DUNCAN HINES® Moist Deluxe® Butter Recipe Golden Cake Mix
3 eggs
1 cup (8 ounces) dairy sour cream
⅔ cup cream of coconut
¼ cup (½ stick) butter or margarine, softened
2 containers (16 ounces each) DUNCAN HINES® Coconut Frosting

1. Preheat oven to 375°F. Place paper liners in 36 (2½-inch) muffin cups.

2. Combine cake mix, eggs, sour cream, cream of coconut and butter in large bowl. Beat at low speed with electric mixer until blended. Beat at medium speed 4 minutes. Fill paper liners half full. Bake at 375°F for 17 to 19 minutes or until toothpick inserted into center comes out clean. Cool in pans 5 minutes. Remove to cooling racks. Cool completely.

3. Frost cupcakes. *Makes 36 cupcakes*

Pretty-in-Pink Peppermint Cupcakes

Peachy Oat Bran Muffins

- 1½ cups oat bran
- ½ cup all-purpose flour
- ⅓ cup firmly packed brown sugar
- 2 teaspoons baking powder
- 1 teaspoon cinnamon
- ½ teaspoon salt
- ¾ cup lowfat milk
- 1 egg, beaten
- ¼ cup vegetable oil
- 1 can (15 ounces) DEL MONTE® LITE® Yellow Cling Sliced Peaches, drained and chopped
- ⅓ cup chopped walnuts
- Granulated sugar (optional)

1. Preheat oven to 425°F. Combine oat bran, flour, brown sugar, baking powder, cinnamon and salt; mix well.

2. Combine milk, egg and oil. Add to dry ingredients; stir just enough to blend. Fold in fruit and nuts.

3. Fill greased muffin cups with batter. Sprinkle with granulated sugar, if desired.

4. Bake 20 to 25 minutes or until golden brown.

Makes 12 medium muffins

Hint: Muffins can be frozen and reheated in microwave or toaster oven.

Prep Time: 10 minutes
Bake Time: 25 minutes

Brunchtime Sour Cream Cupcakes

- 1 cup (2 sticks) butter, softened
- 2 cups plus 4 teaspoons sugar, divided
- 2 eggs
- 1 cup sour cream
- 1 teaspoon almond extract
- 2 cups all-purpose flour
- 1 teaspoon salt
- ½ teaspoon baking soda
- 1 cup chopped walnuts
- 1½ teaspoons ground cinnamon
- ⅛ teaspoon ground nutmeg

1. Preheat oven to 350°F. Lightly grease 18 standard (2½-inch) muffin pan cups or line with paper baking cups.

2. Beat butter and 2 cups sugar in large bowl. Add eggs, one at a time, beating well after each addition. Blend in sour cream and almond extract. Combine flour, salt and baking soda in medium bowl. Add to butter mixture; mix well.

3. Stir together remaining 4 teaspoons sugar, walnuts, cinnamon and nutmeg in small bowl.

4. Fill prepared muffin cups ⅓ full with batter; sprinkle evenly with ⅔ of walnut mixture. Cover with remaining batter. Sprinkle with remaining walnut mixture.

5. Bake 25 to 30 minutes or until toothpick inserted into centers come out clean. Remove cupcakes from pan; cool on wire rack.

Makes 1½ dozen cupcakes

Peachy Oat Bran Muffins

Chocolate Peanut Butter Cups

- **1 package DUNCAN HINES® Moist Deluxe® Swiss Chocolate Cake Mix**
- **1 container DUNCAN HINES® Creamy Home-Style Classic Vanilla Frosting**
- **½ cup creamy peanut butter**
- **15 miniature peanut butter cup candies, wrappers removed, cut in half vertically**

1. Preheat oven to 350°F. Place paper liners in 30 (2½-inch) muffin cups.

2. Prepare, bake and cool cupcakes following package directions for basic recipe.

3. Combine Vanilla frosting and peanut butter in medium bowl. Stir until smooth. Frost one cupcake. Decorate with peanut butter cup candy, cut side down. Repeat with remaining cupcakes, frosting and candies. *Makes 30 servings*

Tip: You can substitute Duncan Hines® Moist Deluxe® Devil's Food, Dark Chocolate Fudge or Butter Recipe Fudge Cake Mix flavors for Swiss Chocolate Cake Mix.

Honey Muffins

- **1 can (8 ounces) DOLE® Crushed Pineapple**
- **1½ cups wheat bran cereal (not flakes)**
- **⅔ cup buttermilk**
- **1 egg, lightly beaten**
- **⅓ cup chopped pecans or walnuts**
- **3 tablespoons vegetable oil**
- **½ cup honey, divided**
- **⅔ cup whole wheat flour**
- **½ teaspoon baking soda**
- **⅛ teaspoon salt**

Combine undrained crushed pineapple, cereal and buttermilk in large bowl. Let stand 10 minutes until cereal has absorbed liquid. Stir in egg, pecans, oil and ¼ cup honey. Combine flour, baking soda and salt in small bowl. Stir into bran mixture until just moistened. Spoon one-half batter into prepared 6 cups,* filling to the top.

Microwave at HIGH (100%) for 3½ to 4 minutes, rotating pan ½ turn after 1½ minutes. Muffins are done when they look dry and set on top. Remove from oven; immediately spoon 1 teaspoon of remaining honey over each muffin. Remove to cooling rack after honey has been absorbed. Repeat procedure with remaining batter and honey. Serve warm. *Makes 12 muffins*

**Line six microwavable muffin cups or six 6-ounce microwavable custard cups with double thickness paper baking cups. (Outer cup will absorb moisture so inner cup sticks to cooked muffin.)*

Chocolate Peanut Butter Cups

Apricot-Peanut Butter Muffins

1¾ cups all-purpose flour
2½ tablespoons sugar
2½ teaspoons baking powder
¾ teaspoon salt
¼ cup CRISCO® all-vegetable shortening
¼ cup JIF® Creamy Peanut Butter
2 eggs
¾ cup milk
2 tablespoons SMUCKER'S® Apricot Preserves

Preheat oven to 400°F. Grease 10 large muffin cups.

Combine flour, sugar, baking powder and salt; cut in shortening and JIF® peanut butter.

Mix eggs and milk together and add all at once to dry ingredients. Stir only until dry ingredients are moistened.

Fill muffin cups ⅔ full. Spoon about ½ teaspoon preserves in center of each muffin.

Bake for 25 minutes or until done.

Makes 10 muffins

Variation: Substitute your favorite SMUCKER'S® flavors in place of the apricot preserves in the above recipe. Experiment with strawberry, blackberry, or even apple butter.

Golden Apple Cupcakes

1 package (18 to 20 ounces) yellow cake mix
1 cup MOTT'S® Chunky Apple Sauce
⅓ cup vegetable oil
3 eggs
¼ cup firmly packed light brown sugar
¼ cup chopped walnuts
½ teaspoon ground cinnamon
Vanilla Frosting (recipe follows)

Heat oven to 350°F. In bowl, combine cake mix, apple sauce, oil and eggs; blend according to package directions. Spoon batter into 24 paper-lined muffin pan cups. Mix brown sugar, walnuts and cinnamon; sprinkle over prepared batter in muffin cups. Bake 20 to 25 minutes or until toothpick inserted in centers comes out clean. Cool in pan 10 minutes. Remove from pan; cool completely on wire rack. Frost cupcakes with Vanilla Frosting.

Makes 24 cupcakes

Vanilla Frosting: In large bowl, beat 1 package (8 ounces) softened cream cheese until light and creamy; blend in ¼ teaspoon vanilla extract. Beat ½ cup heavy cream until stiff; fold into cream cheese mixture.

Apricot-Peanut Butter Muffins

Fudgey Chocolate Cupcakes

- **¾ cup water**
- **½ cup (1 stick) 60% vegetable oil spread, melted**
- **2 egg whites, slightly beaten**
- **1 teaspoon vanilla extract**
- **2¼ cups HERSHEY®S Basic Cocoa Baking Mix (recipe follows)**
- **2 teaspoons powdered sugar**
- **2 teaspoons HERSHEY®S Cocoa (optional)**

1. Heat oven to 350°F. Line 16 muffin cups (2½ inches in diameter) with foil or paper baking cups.

2. Stir together water, melted spread, egg whites and vanilla in large bowl. Add Basic Cocoa Baking Mix; beat on low speed of mixer until blended. Fill muffin cups ⅔ full with batter.

3. Bake 20 to 25 minutes or until wooden pick inserted into centers comes out clean. Remove from pans to wire racks. Cool completely. Sift powdered sugar over tops of cupcakes. If desired, partially cover part of each cupcake with paper cutout. Sift cocoa over exposed powdered sugar. Carefully lift off cutout. Store, covered, at room temperature. *Makes 16 cupcakes*

Hershey®s Basic Cocoa Baking Mix: Stir together 4½ cups all-purpose flour, 2¾ cups sugar, 1¼ cups HERSHEY®S Cocoa, 1 tablespoon plus ½ teaspoon baking powder, 1¾ teaspoons salt and 1¼ teaspoons baking soda. Store in airtight container in cool, dry place for up to 1 month. Stir before using. Makes 8 cups mix.

Chunky Apple Molasses Muffins

- **2 cups all-purpose flour**
- **¼ cup sugar**
- **1 tablespoon baking powder**
- **1 teaspoon ground cinnamon**
- **¼ teaspoon salt**
- **1 Fuji apple, peeled, cored and finely chopped**
- **½ cup milk**
- **¼ cup vegetable oil**
- **¼ cup molasses**
- **1 large egg**

1. Heat oven to 450°F. Lightly grease eight 3-inch muffin pan cups. In large bowl, combine flour, sugar, baking powder, cinnamon and salt. Add apple and stir to distribute evenly.

2. In small bowl, beat together milk, oil, molasses and egg. Stir into dry ingredients and mix just until blended. Fill muffin pan cups with batter. Bake 5 minutes. Reduce heat to 350°F; bake 12 to 15 minutes longer or until centers of muffins spring back when gently pressed. Cool in pan 5 minutes. Remove muffins from pan and cool slightly; serve warm. *Makes 8 (3-inch) muffins*

Favorite recipe from **Washington Apple Commission**

Fudgey Chocolate Cupcakes

Cranberry Cheesecake Muffins

1 package (3 ounces) cream cheese, softened
4 tablespoons sugar, divided
1 cup reduced-fat (2%) milk
⅓ cup vegetable oil
1 egg
1 package (about 15 ounces) cranberry quick bread mix

1. Preheat oven to 400°F. Grease 12 muffin pan cups.

2. Beat cream cheese and 2 tablespoons sugar in small bowl until well blended; set aside.

3. Beat milk, oil and egg in large bowl until blended. Stir in quick bread mix just until dry ingredients are moistened.

4. Fill prepared muffin cups ¼ full with batter. Drop 1 teaspoon cream cheese mixture into center of each cup. Spoon remaining batter over cream cheese mixture.

5. Sprinkle batter with remaining 2 tablespoons sugar. Bake 17 to 22 minutes or until golden brown. Cool 5 minutes. Remove from muffin cups to wire rack to cool. *Makes 12 muffins*

Prep and Bake Time: 30 minutes

Whole Wheat Herb Muffins

1 cup all-purpose flour
1 cup whole wheat flour
⅓ cup sugar
2 teaspoons baking powder
½ teaspoon baking soda
½ teaspoon salt
½ teaspoon dried basil leaves
¼ teaspoon dried marjoram leaves
¼ teaspoon dried oregano leaves
⅛ teaspoon dried thyme leaves
¾ cup raisins
1 cup buttermilk
2 tablespoons butter, melted
1 egg, beaten
2 tablespoons toasted wheat germ

1. Preheat oven to 400°F. Grease 12 (2½-inch) muffin cups.

2. Combine flours, sugar, baking powder, baking soda, salt, basil, marjoram, oregano, thyme and raisins in large bowl. Combine buttermilk, butter and egg in small bowl; stir into flour mixture just until moistened. Spoon evenly into prepared muffin cups. Sprinkle wheat germ over tops of muffins.

3. Bake 15 to 20 minutes or until lightly browned and toothpick inserted in center comes out clean. Remove from pan. Serve warm.

Makes 12 muffins

Cranberry Cheesecake Muffins

Grandma's® Bran Muffins

- 2½ cups bran flakes, divided
- 1 cup raisins
- 1 cup boiling water
- 2 cups buttermilk
- 1 cup GRANDMA'S® Molasses
- ½ cup canola oil
- 2 eggs, beaten
- 2¾ cups all-purpose flour
- 2½ teaspoons baking soda
- ½ teaspoon salt

Heat oven to 400°F. In medium bowl, mix 1 cup bran flakes, raisins and water. Set aside. In large bowl, combine remaining ingredients. Stir in bran-raisin mixture. Pour into greased muffin pan cups. Fill ⅔ full and bake for 20 minutes. Remove muffins and place on rack to cool.

Makes 48 muffins

Quick Tip

To prevent raisins from sinking to the bottom of a muffin batter, toss them with a little of the flour used in the recipe. If the raisins are clumped together, separate them with your fingers, making sure all raisins are coated with flour.

Wisconsin Blue Cheese Muffins

- 2 cups all-purpose flour
- 3 tablespoons sugar
- 1 tablespoon baking powder
- ¼ teaspoon salt
- 1 cup Wisconsin Blue cheese, crumbled
- 1 egg, beaten
- 1 cup milk
- ¼ cup (½ stick) butter, melted

Preheat oven to 400°F. Butter 10 (2½-inch) muffin cups.

Combine flour, sugar, baking powder, salt and cheese in large bowl. Combine egg, milk and butter in small bowl until blended; stir into flour mixture just until moistened. Spoon into prepared muffin cups, filling ¾ full.

Bake 20 to 25 minutes or until golden brown. Remove from pan. Serve warm.

Makes 10 muffins

Favorite recipe from **Wisconsin Milk Marketing Board**

Grandma's® Bran Muffins

Decadent Cakes

Refreshing Lemon Cake

1 package DUNCAN HINES® Moist Deluxe® Butter Recipe Golden Cake Mix
1 container DUNCAN HINES® Creamy Home-Style Cream Cheese Frosting
¾ cup purchased lemon curd
Lemon drop candies, crushed for garnish (optional)

1. Preheat oven to 375°F. Grease and flour two 8- or 9-inch round cake pans.

2. Prepare, bake and cool cakes following package directions for basic recipe.

3. To assemble, place one cake layer on serving plate. Place ¼ cup Cream Cheese frosting in small resealable plastic bag. Snip off one corner. Pipe a bead of frosting on top of layer around outer edge. Fill remaining area with lemon curd. Top with second cake layer. Spread remaining frosting on side and top of cake. Garnish top of cake with crushed lemon candies, if desired.

Makes 12 to 16 servings

Tip: You can substitute Duncan Hines® Vanilla or Vanilla Buttercream Frosting for the Cream Cheese Frosting, if desired.

Refreshing Lemon Cake

Easy Cream Cake

1 package DUNCAN HINES® Moist Deluxe® Classic White Cake Mix
3 egg whites
1⅓ cups half-and-half
2 tablespoons vegetable oil
1 cup flaked coconut, finely chopped
½ cup finely chopped pecans
2 containers DUNCAN HINES® Creamy Home-Style Cream Cheese Frosting

1. Preheat oven to 350°F. Grease and flour three 8-inch round cake pans.

2. Combine cake mix, egg whites, half-and-half, oil, coconut and pecans in large bowl. Beat at low speed with electric mixer until moistened. Beat at medium speed 2 minutes. Pour into prepared pans. Bake at 350°F for 22 to 25 minutes or until toothpick inserted in center comes out clean. Cool following package directions.

3. To assemble, place one cake layer on serving plate. Spread with ¾ cup Cream Cheese frosting. Place second cake layer on top. Spread with ¾ cup frosting. Top with third layer. Spread ¾ cup frosting on top only. Garnish as desired.

Makes 12 to 16 servings

Tip: Spread leftover frosting between two graham crackers for an easy snack.

Sinfully Simple Chocolate Cake

1 package (18¼ ounces) chocolate cake mix plus ingredients to prepare mix
1 cup whipping cream, chilled
⅓ cup chocolate syrup
Fresh fruit for garnish (optional)

1. Prepare cake mix according to package directions for two 8- or 9-inch layers. Cool completely.

2. Beat whipping cream with electric mixer at high speed until it begins to thicken. Gradually add chocolate syrup; beat until soft peaks form.

3. To assemble, place one cake layer on serving plate; spread with half of chocolate whipped cream. Place second cake layer on top; spread with remaining chocolate whipped cream. Garnish, if desired. Store in refrigerator.

Makes 12 servings

Easy Cream Cake

Double Chocolate Bundt Cake

- 1 package (about 18 ounces) chocolate cake mix
- 1 package (4-serving size) instant chocolate pudding mix
- 4 eggs, beaten
- ¾ cup water
- ¾ cup sour cream
- ½ cup oil
- 6 ounces (1 cup) semisweet chocolate chips
- Powdered sugar

1. Preheat oven to 350°F. Spray 10-inch Bundt or tube pan with nonstick cooking spray.

2. Beat cake mix, pudding mix, eggs, water, sour cream and oil in large bowl with electric mixer at medium speed until ingredients are blended. Stir in chocolate chips; pour into prepared pan.

3. Bake 55 to 60 minutes or until cake springs back when lightly touched. Cool 1 hour in pan on wire rack. Invert cake onto serving plate; cool completely. Sprinkle with powdered sugar before serving. *Makes 10 to 12 servings*

Chocolate Chip Cookie Cake

- 1 package DUNCAN HINES® Moist Deluxe® Yellow Cake Mix
- 1 package (4-serving size) vanilla-flavor instant pudding and pie filling mix
- 4 eggs
- 1 cup water
- ⅓ cup vegetable oil
- 1 package (12 ounces) semisweet chocolate chips
- 1½ cups finely chopped pecans
- Confectioners' sugar for garnish

1. Preheat oven to 350°F. Grease and flour 10-inch Bundt pan.

2. Combine cake mix, pudding mix, eggs, water and oil in large mixing bowl. Beat at medium speed with electric mixer for 2 minutes. Stir in chocolate chips and pecans. Pour into prepared pan. Bake at 350°F for 50 to 60 minutes or until toothpick inserted in center comes out clean. Cool in pan 25 minutes. Invert onto serving plate. Cool completely. Dust with confectioners' sugar, if desired. *Makes 12 to 16 servings*

Double Chocolate Bundt Cake

Strawberry Celebration Cake

1 package DUNCAN HINES® Moist Deluxe® Strawberry Supreme Cake Mix
1 cup strawberry preserves, heated
1 container DUNCAN HINES® Creamy Home-Style Cream Cheese Frosting
Strawberry halves for garnish
Mint leaves for garnish

1. Preheat oven to 350°F. Grease and flour 10-inch Bundt or tube pan.

2. Prepare, bake and cool cake following package directions for basic recipe.

3. Split cake horizontally into three even layers. Place bottom cake layer on serving plate. Spread with ½ cup warm preserves. Repeat layering. Top with remaining cake layer. Frost cake with Cream Cheese frosting. Garnish with strawberry halves and mint leaves. Refrigerate until ready to serve.

Makes 12 to 16 servings

Tip: For a delicious variation, substitute 1 cup seedless red raspberry jam for the strawberry preserves.

Aunt Ruth's Favorite White Cake

1 package (18¼ ounces) white cake mix
1¼ cups water
3 eggs
2 tablespoons vegetable oil
1 teaspoon vanilla
½ teaspoon almond extract
Creamy White Frosting (recipe follows)

1. Preheat oven to 350°F. Grease and flour two 8- or 9-inch round cake pans.

2. Combine cake mix, water, eggs and oil in large bowl. Beat at medium speed of electric mixer until well blended. Add vanilla and almond extract; mix until well blended. Divide batter evenly between prepared pans.

3. Bake 30 to 35 minutes or until toothpick inserted into centers come out clean. Cool in pans on wire racks 10 minutes. Remove cakes from pans to racks; cool completely.

4. Prepare Creamy White Frosting. Fill and frost cake with frosting. *Makes one 2-layer cake*

Creamy White Frosting

1 cup milk
3 tablespoons all-purpose flour
1 cup (2 sticks) butter, softened
1 cup powdered sugar
1 teaspoon vanilla

1. Combine milk and flour in medium saucepan; cook and stir over low heat until thickened. Cool.

2. Beat butter in large bowl until creamy. Add powdered sugar; beat until fluffy. Blend in vanilla. Add flour mixture; beat until thick and smooth.

Strawberry Celebration Cake

Double Chocolate Snack Cake

1 package DUNCAN HINES® Moist Deluxe® Devil's Food Cake Mix
1 cup white chocolate chips, divided
½ cup semisweet chocolate chips

1. Preheat oven to 350°F. Grease and flour 13×9-inch pan.

2. Prepare cake mix as directed on package. Stir in ½ cup white chocolate chips and semisweet chocolate chips. Pour into prepared pan. Bake at 350°F for 35 to 40 minutes or until toothpick inserted in center comes out clean. Remove from oven; sprinkle top with remaining ½ cup white chocolate chips. Serve warm or cool completely in pan. *Makes 12 to 16 servings*

Tip: For a special dessert, serve cake warm with a scoop of vanilla ice cream or whipped cream garnished with the chocolate chips.

Butter Pecan Banana Cake

Cake

1 package DUNCAN HINES® Moist Deluxe® Butter Recipe Golden Cake Mix
4 eggs
1 cup mashed ripe bananas (about 3 medium)
¾ cup vegetable oil
½ cup granulated sugar
¼ cup milk
1 teaspoon vanilla extract
1 cup chopped pecans

Frosting

1 cup coarsely chopped pecans
¼ cup (½ stick) butter or margarine
1 container DUNCAN HINES® Vanilla Frosting

1. Preheat oven to 325°F. Grease and flour 10-inch Bundt or tube pan.

2. For cake, combine cake mix, eggs, bananas, oil, sugar, milk and vanilla extract in large mixing bowl. Beat at low speed with electric mixer until moistened. Beat at medium speed for 2 minutes. Stir in 1 cup chopped pecans. Pour into prepared pan. Bake 50 to 60 minutes or until toothpick inserted in center comes out clean. Cool in pan 25 minutes. Invert onto cooling rack. Cool completely.

3. For frosting, place 1 cup coarsely chopped pecans and butter in skillet. Cook on medium heat, stirring until pecans are toasted. Combine nut mixture and frosting in small bowl. Cool until spreading consistency. Frost cake.

Makes 12 to 16 servings

Double Chocolate Snack Cake

Orange Glazed Pound Cake

1 package DUNCAN HINES® Moist Deluxe® Butter Recipe Golden Cake Mix
4 eggs
1 cup sour cream
⅓ cup vegetable oil
¼ cup plus 1 to 2 tablespoons orange juice, divided
2 tablespoons grated orange peel
1 cup confectioners' sugar

1. Preheat oven to 375°F. Grease and flour 10-inch tube pan.

2. Combine cake mix, eggs, sour cream, oil, ¼ cup orange juice and orange peel in large bowl. Beat at medium speed with electric mixer for 2 minutes. Pour into prepared pan. Bake at 375°F for 45 to 50 minutes or until toothpick inserted in center comes out clean. Cool in pan 25 minutes. Invert onto cooling rack. Cool completely.

3. Combine sugar and remaining 1 to 2 tablespoons orange juice in small bowl; stir until smooth. Drizzle over cake. Garnish as desired. *Makes 12 to 16 servings*

Lemon Crumb Cake

1 package DUNCAN HINES® Moist Deluxe® Lemon Supreme Cake Mix
3 eggs
1⅓ cups water
⅓ cup vegetable oil
1 cup all-purpose flour
½ cup packed light brown sugar
½ teaspoon baking powder
½ cup (1 stick) butter or margarine

1. Preheat oven to 350°F. Grease and flour 13×9-inch pan.

2. Combine cake mix, eggs, water and oil in large mixing bowl. Beat at medium speed with electric mixer for 2 minutes. Pour into prepared pan. Combine flour, sugar and baking powder in small bowl. Cut in butter until crumbly. Sprinkle evenly over batter. Bake at 350°F for 35 to 40 minutes or until toothpick inserted in center comes out clean. Cool completely in pan.

Makes 12 to 16 servings

Tip: Butter or margarine will cut more easily into the flour mixture if it is chilled. Use two knives or a pastry cutter to cut the mixture into crumbs.

Orange Glazed Pound Cake

Blueberry Angel Food Cake Rolls

- **1 package DUNCAN HINES® Angel Food Cake Mix**
- **¼ cup confectioners' sugar plus additional for dusting towels**
- **1 can (21 ounces) blueberry pie filling**
- **Mint leaves for garnish (optional)**

1. Preheat oven to 350°F. Line two 15½×10½×1-inch jelly-roll pans with aluminum foil.

2. Prepare cake mix as directed on package. Divide and spread evenly into prepared pans. Cut through batter with knife or spatula to remove large air bubbles. Bake at 350°F for 15 minutes or until set. Invert cakes at once onto clean, lint-free dishtowels dusted with confectioners' sugar. Remove foil carefully. Roll up each cake with towel jelly-roll fashion, starting at short end. Cool completely.

3. Unroll cakes. Spread about 1 cup blueberry pie filling to within 1 inch of edges on each cake. Reroll and place seam-side down on serving plate. Dust with ¼ cup confectioners' sugar. Garnish with mint leaves, if desired.

Makes 2 cakes (8 servings each)

Tip: For a variation in flavor, substitute cherry pie filling for the blueberry pie filling.

Della Robbia Cake

- **1 package DUNCAN HINES® Angel Food Cake Mix**
- **1½ teaspoons grated lemon peel**
- **1 cup water**
- **6 tablespoons granulated sugar**
- **1½ tablespoons cornstarch**
- **1 tablespoon lemon juice**
- **½ teaspoon vanilla extract**
- **Few drops red food coloring**
- **6 cling peach slices**
- **6 medium strawberries, sliced**

1. Preheat oven to 375°F.

2. Prepare cake mix as directed on package, adding lemon peel. Bake and cool cake as directed on package.

3. Combine water, sugar and cornstarch in small saucepan. Cook on medium-high heat until mixture thickens and clears. Remove from heat. Stir in lemon juice, vanilla extract and food coloring.

4. Alternate peach slices with strawberry slices around top of cake. Pour glaze over fruit and top of cake. *Makes 12 to 16 servings*

Tip: For angel food cakes, always use a totally grease-free cake pan to get the best volume.

Blueberry Angel Food Cake Roll

Boston Cream Pie

1 package DUNCAN HINES® Moist Deluxe® Classic Yellow Cake Mix
2 containers (3½ ounces each) ready-to-eat vanilla pudding
1 container DUNCAN HINES® Chocolate Frosting

1. Preheat oven to 350°F. Grease and flour two 8- or 9-inch round pans.

2. Prepare, bake and cool cakes following package directions for basic recipe.

3. To assemble pie, place one cake on serving plate. Spread contents of 2 containers of vanilla pudding on top of cake. Place second cake on filling. Remove lid and foil top from Chocolate frosting container. Heat in microwave oven at HIGH (100% power) for 25 to 30 seconds. Stir. (Mixture should be thin.) Spread the chocolate glaze over top of second cake layer. Refrigerate until ready to serve.

Makes 12 to 16 servings

Tip: For a richer flavor, substitute Duncan Hines® Butter Recipe Golden Cake Mix in place of Yellow Cake Mix.

Chocolate Sprinkle Angel Food Cake

1 package DUNCAN HINES® Angel Food Cake Mix
3 tablespoons chocolate sprinkles

1. Remove top rack from oven; move remaining rack to lowest position. Preheat oven to 350°F.

2. Prepare batter following package directions. Fold in chocolate sprinkles. Pour batter into *ungreased* 10-inch tube pan. Bake and cool following package directions.

Makes 12 to 16 servings

For a quick finish, simply dust this cake with confectioners' sugar.

Boston Cream Pie

Take-Along Cake

1 package DUNCAN HINES® Moist Deluxe® Swiss Chocolate Cake Mix
1 package (12 ounces) semisweet chocolate chips
1 cup miniature marshmallows
¼ cup (½ stick) butter or margarine, melted
½ cup packed brown sugar
½ cup chopped pecans or walnuts

1. Preheat oven to 350°F. Grease and flour 13×9-inch pan.

2. Prepare cake mix as directed on package. Add chocolate chips and marshmallows to batter. Pour into prepared pan. Drizzle melted butter over batter. Sprinkle with sugar and top with pecans. Bake at 350°F for 45 to 55 minutes or until toothpick inserted in center comes out clean. Serve warm or cool completely in pan.

Makes 12 to 16 servings

Tip: To keep leftover pecans fresh, store them in the freezer in an airtight container.

Banana Fudge Layer Cake

1 package DUNCAN HINES® Moist Deluxe® Yellow Cake Mix
1⅓ cups water
3 eggs
⅓ cup vegetable oil
1 cup mashed ripe bananas (about 3 medium)
1 container DUNCAN HINES® Chocolate Frosting

1. Preheat oven to 350°F. Grease and flour two 9-inch round cake pans.

2. Combine cake mix, water, eggs and oil in large bowl. Beat at low speed with electric mixer until moistened. Beat at medium speed 2 minutes. Stir in bananas.

3. Pour into prepared pans. Bake at 350°F for 28 to 31 minutes or until toothpick inserted in center comes out clean. Cool in pans 15 minutes. Remove from pans; cool completely.

4. Fill and frost cake with frosting. Garnish as desired.

Makes 12 to 16 servings

Cakes

Take-Along Cake

Blueberry Cream Cheese Pound Cake

1 package (16 ounces) pound cake mix, divided
1½ cups fresh blueberries
5 ounces cream cheese, softened
2 eggs
¾ cup milk
Powdered sugar (optional)

1. Preheat oven to 350°F. Grease 9×5×2-inch loaf pan.

2. Place ¼ cup cake mix in medium bowl; add blueberries and toss until well coated.

3. Beat cream cheese in large bowl 1 minute on medium speed of electric mixer until light and fluffy. Add eggs, one at a time, beating well after each addition.

4. Add remaining cake mix alternately with milk, beginning and ending with cake mix, beating well after each addition. Beat 1 minute on medium speed or until light and fluffy.

5. Fold blueberry mixture into batter. Pour mixture into prepared pan. Bake 55 to 60 minutes or until wooden pick inserted into center comes out clean.

6. Cool in pan on wire rack 10 minutes. Remove cake to wire rack; cool completely. Lightly sprinkle top with powdered sugar, if desired.

Makes 1 (9-inch) pound cake

Rich Caramel Cake

1 (14-ounce) package caramels, unwrapped
½ cup (1 stick) butter or margarine
1 (14-ounce) can EAGLE BRAND® Sweetened Condensed Milk (NOT evaporated milk)
1 (18¼- or 18½-ounce) package chocolate cake mix, plus ingredients to prepare mix
1 cup coarsely chopped pecans

1. Preheat oven to 350°F. In heavy saucepan over low heat, melt caramels and butter. Remove from heat; add EAGLE BRAND®. Mix well. Set aside caramel mixture. Prepare cake mix as package directs.

2. Spread 2 cups cake batter into greased 13×9-inch baking pan; bake 15 minutes. Spread caramel mixture evenly over cake; spread remaining cake batter over caramel mixture. Top with pecans. Return to oven; bake 30 to 35 minutes or until cake springs back when lightly touched. Cool. *Makes 10 to 12 servings*

Blueberry Cream Cheese Pound Cake

Dump Cake

1 can (20 ounces) crushed pineapple with juice, undrained
1 can (21 ounces) cherry pie filling
1 package DUNCAN HINES® Moist Deluxe® Yellow Cake Mix
1 cup chopped pecans or walnuts
½ cup (1 stick) butter or margarine, cut into thin slices

1. Preheat oven to 350°F. Grease 13×9-inch pan.

2. Dump pineapple with juice into prepared pan. Spread evenly. Dump in pie filling. Spread evenly. Sprinkle cake mix evenly over cherry layer. Sprinkle pecans over cake mix. Dot with butter. Bake at 350°F for 50 minutes or until top is lightly browned. Serve warm or at room temperature.

Makes 12 to 16 servings

Tip: You can use Duncan Hines® Moist Deluxe® Pineapple Supreme Cake Mix in place of Moist Deluxe® Yellow Cake Mix.

Cinnamon Ripple Cake

1 package DUNCAN HINES® Angel Food Cake Mix
2¼ teaspoons ground cinnamon, divided
1½ cups frozen whipped topping, thawed

1. Preheat oven to 350°F.

2. Prepare cake following package directions. Spoon one third of batter into ungreased 10-inch tube pan. Spread evenly. Sprinkle 1 teaspoon cinnamon over batter with small fine sieve. Repeat. Top with remaining cake batter. Bake and cool following package directions.

3. Combine whipped topping and ¼ teaspoon cinnamon in small bowl. Serve with cake slices.

Makes 12 to 16 servings

To slice a cake, use a serrated knife and cut in a sawing motion.

Cakes

Dump Cake

Butterscotch Bundt Cake

1 package (about 18 ounces) yellow cake mix
1 package (4-serving size) butterscotch-flavored instant pudding mix
1 cup water
3 eggs
2 teaspoons ground cinnamon
½ cup chopped pecans
Powdered sugar (optional)

Preheat oven to 325°F. Spray 10-inch Bundt pan with nonstick cooking spray. Combine all ingredients, except pecans and powdered sugar, in large bowl. Beat with electric mixer at medium-high speed 2 minutes or until blended. Stir in pecans. Pour into prepared pan. Bake 40 to 50 minutes or until cake springs back when lightly touched. Cool on wire rack 10 minutes. Invert cake onto serving plate. Cool completely. Sprinkle with powdered sugar, if desired.

Makes 12 to 16 servings

Variation: Try substituting white cake mix for yellow cake mix, pistachio-flavored pudding mix for the butterscotch-flavored pudding mix and walnuts for pecans for a delicious Pistachio Bundt Cake with Walnuts.

Holiday Coffeecake

2 cups biscuit mix
1 (14-ounce) can EAGLE BRAND® Sweetened Condensed Milk (NOT evaporated milk)
¾ cup sour cream
¼ cup (½ stick) butter or margarine, melted
2 eggs
1½ teaspoons ground cinnamon, divided
½ cup chopped pecans
2 tablespoons firmly packed light brown sugar
1 tablespoon butter or margarine, melted

1. Preheat oven to 350°F. In large mixing bowl, beat biscuit mix, EAGLE BRAND®, sour cream, ¼ cup butter, eggs and ½ teaspoon cinnamon until smooth. Pour batter into lightly greased 11×7-inch baking dish.

2. In small mixing bowl, combine pecans, brown sugar, 1 tablespoon butter and remaining 1 teaspoon cinnamon. Sprinkle mixture evenly over batter. Bake 40 to 45 minutes or until wooden pick inserted in center comes out clean. Cool in dish on wire rack 10 minutes.

Makes 8 servings

Butterscotch Bundt Cake

Chocolate Banana Cake

Cake

1 package DUNCAN HINES® Moist Deluxe® Devil's Food Cake Mix
3 eggs
1⅓ cups milk
½ cup vegetable oil

Topping

1 package (4-serving size) banana cream instant pudding and pie filling mix
1 cup milk
1 cup whipping cream, whipped
1 medium banana
Lemon juice
Chocolate sprinkles for garnish

1. Preheat oven to 350°F. Grease and flour 13×9×2-inch pan.

2. For cake, combine cake mix, eggs, milk and oil in large bowl. Beat at low speed with electric mixer until moistened. Beat at medium speed 2 minutes. Pour into pan. Bake at 350°F for 35 to 38 minutes or until toothpick inserted in center comes out clean. Cool completely.

3. For topping, combine pudding mix and milk in large bowl. Stir until smooth. Fold in whipped cream. Spread on top of cooled cake. Slice banana; dip in lemon juice and arrange on top. Garnish with chocolate sprinkles. Refrigerate until ready to serve.

Makes 12 to 16 servings

Tip: A wire whisk is a great utensil to use when making instant pudding. It quickly eliminates all lumps.

Butter Brickle Cake

⅔ cup sugar
2 teaspoons ground cinnamon
1 package (about 18 ounces) yellow cake mix
1 package (4-serving size) butterscotch-flavored instant pudding mix
4 eggs
¾ cup oil
¾ cup water
1 cup chopped walnuts, divided

1. Preheat oven to 350°F. Grease and flour 13×9-inch cake pan. Combine sugar and cinnamon in small bowl; set aside.

2. Combine cake mix, pudding mix, eggs, oil and water in large bowl. Beat 4 to 5 minutes with electric mixer on medium speed or until batter is fluffy. Pour half of cake batter into prepared pan. Sprinkle ½ cup walnuts evenly on top. Sprinkle with half of cinnamon-sugar mixture. Cover with remaining cake batter. Sprinkle remaining walnuts onto batter. Sprinkle with remaining cinnamon-sugar mixture.

3. Bake 40 to 45 minutes or until toothpick inserted into center comes out clean. Cool completely in pan on wire rack.

Makes 12 to 16 servings

Serving Suggestion: This cake is great served warm from the oven, topped with whipped cream or partially melted vanilla ice cream!

Chocolate Banana Cake

Creamy Cheesecakes

Apple-Pecan Cheesecake

2 packages (8 ounces each) cream cheese, softened
⅔ cup sugar, divided
2 eggs
½ teaspoon vanilla
1 (9-inch) prepared graham cracker pie crust
½ teaspoon ground cinnamon
4 cups Golden Delicious apples, peeled, cored and thinly sliced (about 2½ pounds apples)
½ cup chopped pecans

1. Preheat oven to 350°F.

2. Beat cream cheese and ⅓ cup sugar in large bowl with electric mixer at medium speed until well blended. Add eggs, 1 at a time, beating well after each addition. Blend in vanilla; pour into crust.

3. Combine remaining ⅓ cup sugar and cinnamon in large bowl. Add apples; toss gently to coat. Spoon or arrange apple mixture over cream cheese mixture. Sprinkle with pecans.

4. Bake 1 hour and 10 minutes or until set. Cool completely. Store in refrigerator.

Makes one 9-inch cheesecake

Apple-Pecan Cheesecake

Premier White Lemony Cheesecake

Crust

6 tablespoons butter or margarine, softened
¼ cup granulated sugar
1¼ cups all-purpose flour
1 egg yolk
⅛ teaspoon salt

Filling

6 bars (*two* 6-ounce boxes) NESTLÉ® TOLL HOUSE® Premier White Baking Bars, broken into pieces *or* 2 cups (12-ounce package) NESTLÉ® TOLL HOUSE® Premier White Morsels
½ cup heavy whipping cream
2 packages (8 ounces each) cream cheese, softened
1 tablespoon lemon juice
2 teaspoons grated lemon peel
¼ teaspoon salt
3 egg whites
1 egg

PREHEAT oven to 350°F. Lightly grease 9-inch springform pan.

For Crust

BEAT butter and sugar in small mixer bowl until creamy. Beat in flour, egg yolk and salt. Press mixture onto bottom and 1 inch up side of prepared pan.

BAKE for 14 to 16 minutes or until crust is set.

For Filling

MICROWAVE baking bars and whipping cream in medium, uncovered, microwave-safe bowl on MEDIUM-HIGH (70%) power for 1 minute. STIR. Morsels may retain some of their original shape. If necessary, microwave at additional 10- to 15-second intervals, stirring just until morsels are melted.

BEAT cream cheese, lemon juice, lemon peel and salt in large mixer bowl until smooth. Gradually beat in melted baking bars. Beat in egg whites and egg. Pour into crust.

BAKE for 35 to 40 minutes or until edge is lightly browned. Run knife around edge of cheesecake. Cool completely in pan on wire rack. Refrigerate for several hours or overnight. Remove side of springform pan. Garnish as desired.

Makes 12 to 16 servings

Quick Tip

A picture-perfect cheesecake has a smooth top. Some cheesecakes will have small cracks around the rim; however, there should never be center cracks. Keep in mind that the following factors can contribute to center crack formation: overbaking; baking in too hot of an oven; overbeating the batter; jarring the cake during baking or cooling; refrigerating the cake before it is completely cooled; using the wrong pan size.

Premier White Lemony Cheesecake

Maple Pumpkin Cheesecake

1¼ cups graham cracker crumbs
¼ cup sugar
¼ cup (½ stick) butter or margarine, melted
3 (8-ounce) packages cream cheese, softened
1 (14-ounce) can EAGLE BRAND® Sweetened Condensed Milk (NOT evaporated milk)
1 (15-ounce) can pumpkin
3 eggs
¼ cup maple syrup
1½ teaspoons ground cinnamon
1 teaspoon ground nutmeg
½ teaspoon salt
Maple Pecan Glaze (recipe follows)

1. Preheat oven to 325°F. In small mixing bowl, combine crumbs, sugar and butter; press firmly on bottom of 9-inch springform pan.* In large mixing bowl, beat cream cheese until fluffy. Gradually beat in EAGLE BRAND® until smooth. Add pumpkin, eggs, maple syrup, cinnamon, nutmeg and salt; mix well. Pour into prepared pan. Bake 1 hour 15 minutes or until center appears nearly set when shaken. Cool 1 hour. Cover and chill at least 4 hours.

2. To serve, spoon some Maple Pecan Glaze over cheesecake. Garnish with whipped cream and pecans, if desired. Pass remaining sauce. Store leftovers covered in refrigerator.

Makes one 9-inch cheesecake

**To use 13×9-inch baking pan, press crumb mixture firmly on bottom of pan. Proceed as directed, except bake 50 to 60 minutes or until center appears nearly set when shaken.*

Maple Pecan Glaze: In medium saucepan over medium-high heat, combine ¾ cup maple syrup and 1 cup (½ pint) whipping cream; bring to a boil. Boil rapidly 15 to 20 minutes or until thickened, stirring occasionally. Add ½ cup chopped pecans.

Prep Time: 25 minutes
Bake Time: 1 hour and 15 minutes
Cool Time: 1 hour
Chill Time: 4 hours

Maple Pumpkin Cheesecake

Chocolate Sour Cream Cheesecake

Chocolate Crumb Crust (recipe follows)
3 packages (8 ounces each) fat-free cream cheese, softened
1 cup reduced-fat sour cream
2 eggs
¼ cup fat-free chocolate syrup
⅔ cup sugar
⅓ cup unsweetened cocoa powder
3 tablespoons all-purpose flour

1. Preheat oven to 350°F. Prepare Chocolate Crumb Crust; set aside. Beat cream cheese in large bowl with electric mixer at high speed until fluffy. Beat in sour cream until smooth. Beat in eggs, 1 at a time. Mix in chocolate syrup, sugar, cocoa and flour until smooth. Pour over crust.

2. Bake 50 to 60 minutes or until set in center. Loosen cheesecake from edge of pan with knife. Cool on wire rack. Cover; refrigerate overnight.

3. Remove side of pan. Garnish cheesecake with dollops of nonfat whipped topping, chocolate shavings and chocolate curls, if desired.

Makes 12 servings

Chocolate Crumb Crust

1¼ cups graham cracker crumbs
2 tablespoons sugar
2 tablespoons unsweetened cocoa powder
¼ cup (½ stick) margarine, melted

1. Preheat oven to 350°F. Combine graham cracker crumbs, sugar and cocoa in bottom of 9-inch springform pan; stir in margarine. Pat mixture evenly onto bottom and 1 inch up side of pan.

2. Bake 8 minutes or until lightly browned. Cool on wire rack.

Makes 1 (9-inch) crust

Quick Tip

To make chocolate curls, melt 7 (1-ounce) squares of semisweet chocolate in a small bowl over hot water, stirring often. Pour the melted chocolate onto a cold baking sheet and spread out into a 6×4-inch rectangle. Refrigerate just until set, about 15 minutes. Pull the longer edge of a metal spatula across the surface of the soft chocolate, letting it curl up in front of the spatula. Place the curls on waxed paper.

Chocolate Sour Cream Cheesecake

Mocha Marble Cheesecake

- 12 ounces cream cheese, softened
- ½ cup sugar
- 1 teaspoon vanilla
- 2 eggs
- ½ cup white crème de cacao
- 1 teaspoon instant coffee granules
- 1 (6-ounce) READY CRUST® Graham Cracker Pie Crust

1. Preheat oven to 325°F. Beat cream cheese in medium bowl until smooth. Add sugar and vanilla. Add eggs, one at a time, beating until well blended.

2. Reserve ½ cup cream cheese mixture; set aside. Pour remaining mixture into crust. Mix crème de cacao and coffee granules with reserved cream cheese mixture.

3. Place crust on baking sheet. Pour coffee mixture over cheesecake filling. Gently cut through coffee layer with knife to create marbled appearance. Bake 30 to 35 minutes or until just set in center. Cool on wire rack. Chill 3 hours. Refrigerate leftovers. *Makes 8 servings*

Prep Time: 10 minutes
Bake Time: 30 to 35 minutes
Chill Time: 3 hours

Refreshing Choco-Orange Cheesecake

- 1 cup graham cracker crumbs
- ¼ cup (½ stick) butter or margarine, melted
- 2 cups sugar, divided
- 1 cup HERSHEY®'S Semi-Sweet Chocolate Chips
- 3 packages (8 ounces each) cream cheese, softened
- 4 eggs
- 1½ cups dairy sour cream
- 2 teaspoons orange extract
- 1 teaspoon freshly grated orange peel
- Whipped topping and orange wedges (optional)

1. Stir together graham cracker crumbs, melted butter and ¼ cup sugar in small bowl; pat firmly onto bottom of 9-inch springform pan.

2. Place chocolate chips in medium microwave-safe bowl. Microwave at HIGH (100%) 1 minute or just until chips are melted when stirred.

3. Beat cream cheese and remaining 1¾ cups sugar in large bowl; add eggs, one at a time, beating after each addition. Stir in sour cream and orange extract. Stir 3 cups cream cheese mixture into melted chocolate chips; pour into crust. Freeze 10 to 15 minutes or until chocolate sets.

4. Heat oven to 325°F. Stir orange peel into remaining cream cheese mixture; gently spread over chocolate mixture.

5. Bake 1 hour 15 minutes or until set except for 3-inch circle in center; turn off oven. Let stand in oven, with door ajar, 1 hour; remove from oven. With knife, loosen cheesecake from side of pan. Cool completely; remove side of pan. Cover; refrigerate. Garnish with whipped topping and orange wedges, if desired. *Makes 12 servings*

Chocolate Turtle Cheesecake

Cheesecake

24 chocolate sandwich cookies, ground (about 2¾ cups)
2 tablespoons butter or margarine, melted
2 packages (8 ounces each) cream cheese, softened
⅓ cup sugar
¼ cup sour cream
2 eggs
1 teaspoon vanilla

Caramel Sauce

15 caramels (⅓ of 15-ounce package)
⅓ cup milk

Fudge Sauce

¼ cup whipping cream
1 tablespoon butter or margarine
¼ cup sugar
Dash salt
¼ cup unsweetened cocoa powder, sifted
½ cup pecan halves

1. For cheesecake, preheat oven to 350°F. Combine ground cookies and butter in medium bowl; pat evenly on bottom and 1 inch up side of 9-inch springform pan. Place in freezer while preparing filling.

2. Beat cream cheese in large bowl with electric mixer at medium speed until fluffy. Beat in sugar, sour cream, eggs and vanilla until smooth. Pour mixture into prepared crust.

3. Bake cheesecake 30 to 35 minutes or until almost set in center. Cool on wire rack. Refrigerate, loosely covered, 8 hours or up to 3 days.

4. For caramel sauce, heat caramel candies and milk in small saucepan over medium-low heat until melted, stirring frequently. Cover and refrigerate up to 3 days.

5. For fudge sauce, heat whipping cream and butter in small saucepan over medium heat until butter is melted, stirring frequently. Stir in sugar and salt; cook until sugar is dissolved, stirring frequently. Reduce heat to low; whisk in cocoa. Cover and refrigerate up to 3 days.

6. Just before serving, reheat sauces. Remove side of springform pan from cheesecake, then place on a serving plate. Drizzle sauces over cheesecake. Top each serving with 2 to 3 pecan halves.

Makes 12 servings

Chocolate Chip Cheesecake

Crust

- 1½ cups (about 15) crushed chocolate sandwich cookies
- 2 tablespoons butter or margarine, melted
- 2 cups (12-ounce package) NESTLÉ® TOLL HOUSE® Semi-Sweet Chocolate Mini Morsels, *divided*

Filling

- 2 packages (8 ounces each) cream cheese, softened
- ½ cup granulated sugar
- 1 tablespoon vanilla extract
- 2 eggs
- 2 tablespoons all-purpose flour
- ¾ cup NESTLÉ® CARNATION® Evaporated Milk
- ½ cup sour cream

For Crust

PREHEAT oven to 300°F.

COMBINE cookie crumbs with butter in medium bowl until moistened; press onto bottom of ungreased 9-inch springform pan. Sprinkle with 1 *cup* morsels.

For Filling

BEAT cream cheese, sugar and vanilla extract in large mixer bowl until smooth. Beat in eggs and flour. Gradually beat in evaporated milk and sour cream. Pour over crust. Sprinkle with *remaining* morsels.

BAKE for 25 minutes. Cover loosely with aluminum foil. Bake for additional 30 to 40 minutes or until edge is set but center still moves slightly. Place in refrigerator immediately; refrigerate for 2 hours or until firm. Remove side of springform pan. *Makes 12 to 14 servings*

Note: Cheesecake may be baked in 13×9-inch pan. Prepare as above. Bake in preheated 300°F. oven for 20 minutes. Cover loosely with aluminum foil. Bake for additional 20 to 30 minutes.

Sweet Potato Cheesecake

- 2 packages (8 ounces each) cream cheese, softened
- ¼ cup sugar
- ¼ cup packed brown sugar
- 1 teaspoon vanilla
- 2 eggs
- 1½ cups sweet potato purée (about 1 pound uncooked potato)
- ½ teaspoon cinnamon
- Pinch *each* ground cloves, ground ginger and ground nutmeg
- 1 (9-inch) graham cracker crust

1. Preheat oven to 350°F. In electric mixer bowl, beat the cream cheese until smooth. Add sugars and vanilla; beat until thoroughly blended. Add the eggs 1 at a time, beating well after each addition. Add sweet potato purée and beat well. Add spices; mix until thoroughly blended.

2. Pour batter into crust. Bake 45 to 50 minutes. Let cool completely before serving.

Makes 8 servings

Chocolate Chip Cheesecake

Chocolate Raspberry Cheesecake

2 (3-ounce) packages cream cheese, softened
1 (14-ounce) can sweetened condensed milk
1 egg
3 tablespoons lemon juice
1 teaspoon vanilla
1 cup fresh or frozen raspberries
1 (6-ounce) READY CRUST® Chocolate Pie Crust
Chocolate Glaze (recipe follows)

1. Preheat oven to 350°F. Beat cream cheese in medium bowl with electric mixer at medium speed until fluffy. Gradually beat in sweetened condensed milk until smooth. Add egg, lemon juice and vanilla; mix well. Arrange raspberries on bottom of crust. Slowly pour cream cheese mixture over raspberries.

2. Bake 30 to 35 minutes or until center is almost set. Cool on wire rack.

3. Prepare Chocolate Glaze; spread over cheesecake. Refrigerate 3 hours. Garnish as desired. Refrigerate leftovers. *Makes 8 servings*

Chocolate Glaze: Melt 2 (1-ounce) squares semisweet baking chocolate with ¼ cup whipping cream in small saucepan over low heat. Cook and stir until thickened and smooth. Remove from heat.

Prep Time: 15 minutes
Bake Time: 30 to 35 minutes
Chilling Time: 3 hours

Strawberry Cheesecake

3 packages (8 ounces each) cream cheese, softened
1 cup no-sugar-added strawberry pourable fruit*
3 teaspoons vanilla, divided
¼ teaspoon salt
4 eggs
1 cup sour cream**
Fresh strawberry halves or slices (optional)

**You can substitute ¾ cup no-sugar-added strawberry fruit spread combined with ¼ cup warm water.*

***Do not use reduced-calorie sour cream.*

Preheat oven to 325°F. Beat cream cheese in large bowl until creamy. Blend in pourable fruit, 1 teaspoon vanilla and salt. Add eggs, one at a time, beating after each addition. Pour into greased 9-inch springform pan. Bake 50 minutes. Combine sour cream and remaining 2 teaspoons vanilla; mix well. Carefully spoon over warm cheesecake. Return to oven; continue baking 10 minutes or just until set. Turn oven off; leave cheesecake in oven, with door closed, 30 minutes. Transfer to wire rack; loosen cheesecake from rim of pan. Cool completely before removing rim. Cover and chill at least 6 hours or overnight. Just before serving, garnish cheesecake with strawberries, if desired. *Makes 10 servings*

Chocolate Raspberry Cheesecake

Chocolate Turtle Cheesecake

24 chocolate sandwich cookies, ground (about 2¾ cups)
2 tablespoons butter, melted
2 packages (8 ounces each) cream cheese, softened
2 eggs
⅓ cup sugar
¼ cup sour cream
1 teaspoon vanilla
½ cup caramel ice cream topping
½ cup hot fudge topping
½ cup pecan halves

1. Preheat oven to 350°F. Combine ground cookies and butter in medium bowl; pat evenly on bottom and 1 inch up side of 9-inch springform pan. Place in freezer while preparing filling.

2. Beat cream cheese in large bowl with electric mixer until fluffy. Beat in eggs, sugar, sour cream and vanilla until smooth. Pour mixture into prepared crust.

3. Bake cheesecake 30 to 35 minutes or until almost set in center. Cool on wire rack. Refrigerate, loosely covered, 8 hours or up to 3 days.

4. To complete recipe, remove side of springform pan from cheesecake; place on serving plate. Drizzle caramel and fudge toppings over cake; cut cake into wedges. Top each serving with 2 to 3 pecan halves. *Makes 12 servings*

Lemon Party Cheesecake

1 (18¼- or 18½-ounce) package yellow cake mix*
4 eggs, divided
¼ cup vegetable oil*
2 (8-ounce) packages cream cheese, softened
1 (14-ounce) can EAGLE BRAND® Sweetened Condensed Milk (NOT evaporated milk)
¼ to ⅓ cup lemon juice from concentrate
2 teaspoons grated lemon peel (optional)
1 teaspoon vanilla extract

**If "pudding added" cake mix is used, decrease oil to 3 tablespoons.*

1. Preheat oven to 300°F. Reserve ½ cup dry cake mix. In large mixing bowl, combine remaining cake mix, 1 egg and oil; mix well (mixture will be crumbly). Press firmly on bottom and 1½ inches up sides of greased 13×9-inch baking pan.

2. In same bowl, beat cream cheese until fluffy. Gradually beat in EAGLE BRAND® until smooth. Add remaining 3 eggs and reserved ½ cup cake mix; beat on medium speed of electric mixer 1 minute. Stir in lemon juice, lemon peel (optional) and vanilla.

3. Pour into crust. Bake 50 to 55 minutes or until center is set. Cool to room temperature. Chill thoroughly. Cut into squares to serve. Garnish as desired. Refrigerate leftovers.

Makes 1 dozen squares

Prep Time: 20 minutes

Chocolate Turtle Cheesecake

Cheesecake 5 Ways

Crumb Crust (recipe follows)
3 packages (8 ounces each) cream cheese, softened
¾ cup sugar
3 eggs
1 teaspoon vanilla extract

1. Prepare Crumb Crust. Heat oven to 350°F.

2. Beat cream cheese and sugar in large bowl until smooth. Add eggs, one at a time, beating well after each addition. Stir in vanilla. Pour into prepared crust.

3. Bake 45 to 50 minutes or until almost set.* Remove from oven to wire rack. With knife, loosen cake from side of pan. Cool completely; remove side of pan.

4. Cover; refrigerate several hours or until chilled. Just before serving, garnish as desired. Cover and refrigerate leftover cheesecake.

Makes 10 to 12 servings

**Cheesecakes are less likely to crack if baked in a water bath.*

Crumb Crust: Heat oven to 350°F. Stir together 1 cup graham cracker crumbs and 2 tablespoons sugar in small bowl; blend in ¼ cup (½ stick) melted butter or margarine, mixing well. Press mixture onto bottom and ½ inch up side of 9-inch springform pan. Bake 8 to 10 minutes. Cool.

Chocolate Cheesecake: Increase sugar to 1¼ cups and add ⅓ cup HERSHEY'S Cocoa. Increase vanilla extract to 1½ teaspoons.

Toffee Bits Cheesecake: Prepare cheesecakes as directed. Stir 1⅓ cups (8-ounce package) HEATH® BITS 'O BRICKLE® Almond Toffee Bits into batter.

Chocolate Chip Cheesecake: Prepare cheesecake as directed. Stir 1 to 1½ cups HERSHEY'S MINI CHIPS™ Semi-Sweet Chocolate Chips into batter.

Mocha Cheesecake: Prepare Chocolate Cheesecake, using HERSHEY'S Dutch Processed Cocoa. Add 1½ teaspoons instant coffee granules to batter.

Mocha Toffee with Chocolate Chips Cheesecake: Prepare Mocha Cheesecake as directed. Stir ¾ cup HEATH® BITS 'O BRICKLE® Toffee Bits and ¾ cup HERSHEY'S MINI CHIPS™ Semi-Sweet Chocolate Chips into batter.

Quick Tip

A simple doneness test is to gently shake a cheesecake—a 1-inch area in center should jiggle slightly. This area will firm during cooling. After baking, run a knife around the inside of the pan to loosen the edges of the crust. Let cool and then remove the rim of the pan. Cheesecakes can be stored in the refrigerator for up to one week, but for the best flavor, bring them to room temperature before serving. Cheesecakes are not recommended for freezing.

Cranberry Swirl Pumpkin Cheesecake

- 2 packages (8 ounces each) cream cheese, softened
- ½ cup sugar
- 1 teaspoon vanilla
- 2 eggs
- 1 can (15 ounces) solid-pack pumpkin
- 1 teaspoon ground cinnamon
- ½ teaspoon ground nutmeg
- ½ teaspoon ground ginger
- ½ teaspoon ground cloves
- Pinch of salt
- 1 (9-inch) graham cracker crust
- 1 (10-ounce) tub frozen cranberry-orange sauce, thawed and puréed in food processor

1. Preheat oven to 350°F. Beat cream cheese, sugar and vanilla in large mixer bowl of electric mixer at medium speed until cream cheese is smooth. Add eggs, 1 at a time, beating well after each addition. Add pumpkin, spices and salt. Mix until well combined.

2. Spread ¾ cup pumpkin mixture evenly into crust. Pour about ⅓ cup cranberry sauce on top of pumpkin mixture. Pour remaining pumpkin mixture into crust and top with remaining cranberry sauce. Swirl cranberry sauce into pumpkin mixture with knife, being careful not to scrape crust.

3. Bake 50 minutes to 1 hour. Cheesecake will not be completely set in the center. Cool completely and refrigerate at least 2 hours or overnight.

Makes 8 servings

Variation: Add ¼ teaspoon salt and an additional 1 teaspoon cinnamon to pumpkin mixture and fold cranberry sauce into pumpkin mixture instead of swirling. Pour into crust and bake as directed above.

Chocolate Cherry Cheesecake

- 1 (8-ounce) package cream cheese, softened
- ¾ cup sugar
- 2 eggs
- 2 (1-ounce) squares semi-sweet chocolate, melted
- 1 teaspoon vanilla
- 1 (6-ounce) READY CRUST® Chocolate Pie Crust
- 1 (21-ounce) can cherry pie filling

1. Preheat oven to 325°F. Beat cream cheese in medium bowl until fluffy. Add sugar, eggs, chocolate and vanilla; mix well. Place crust on baking sheet. Pour mixture into crust.

2. Bake 35 minutes or until filling springs back when touched lightly. Cool on wire rack.

3. Spread cherry pie filling over top. Chill 3 hours. Refrigerate leftovers. *Makes 8 servings*

Prep Time: 15 minutes
Bake Time: 35 minutes
Chill Time: 3 hours

Cranberry Swirl Pumpkin Cheesecake

Strawberry Cheesecake Pie

- 1 *prepared* 9-inch (6 ounces) graham cracker crumb crust
- ⅔ cup (5 fluid-ounce can) NESTLÉ® CARNATION® Evaporated Fat Free Milk
- 1 package (8 ounces) fat free cream cheese, softened
- 1 egg
- ½ cup granulated sugar
- 2 tablespoons all-purpose flour
- 1 teaspoon grated lemon peel
- 1½ to 2 cups halved fresh strawberries
- 3 tablespoons strawberry jelly, warmed

PREHEAT oven to 325°F.

PLACE evaporated milk, cream cheese, egg, sugar, flour and lemon peel in blender; cover. Blend until smooth. Pour into crust.

BAKE for 35 to 40 minutes or until center is set. Cool completely in pan on wire rack. Arrange strawberries on top of pie; drizzle with jelly. Refrigerate well before serving.

Makes 8 servings

Classic Apple Sauce Cheesecake

- 2½ cups bran flakes, divided
- ¾ cup (1½ sticks) butter
- ¼ cup firmly packed light brown sugar
- 2 packages (8 ounces each) cream cheese, softened
- ¾ cup sugar
- 3 eggs
- 2 cups MOTT'S® Apple Sauce, divided
- 1 teaspoon vanilla extract

1. Heat oven to 350°F. Finely roll 2 cups bran flakes. Place crumbs in large bowl; stir in butter and brown sugar. Press mixture firmly on bottom and up side of 9-inch pie plate; set aside. In bowl, beat cream cheese, sugar and eggs until smooth.

2. Stir in 1 cup apple sauce and vanilla; pour into bran crust. Bake 40 to 45 minutes until center is just set. Gently spread remaining 1 cup apple sauce over cheesecake; cool. Chill at least 4 hours. Sprinkle with remaining ½ cup bran before serving.

Makes 10 servings

Quick Tip

Cheesecake is a creamy baked dessert made from cheese that is sweetened and flavored. The texture can range from airy and light to dense and heavy. Some are flawlessly smooth and moist while others have a drier and more crumbly consistency. Traditional cheesecakes are simply flavored with vanilla or lemon and topped with sour cream or berries. The popularity of this rich dessert has spawned countless variations.

Strawberry Cheesecake Pie

Pies, Cobblers, & Tarts

Upside-Down Pear Tart

½ cup sugar
2 tablespoons butter or margarine
2 teaspoons grated lemon peel
5 medium (2½ to 3 pounds) firm USA winter pears, peeled, cored and cut into eighths
1 tablespoon lemon juice
Pastry for 9-inch single crust pie
Vanilla yogurt

Heat sugar over medium heat in heavy 10-inch skillet with oven-safe handle until syrupy and light brown in color. Remove from heat and add butter and lemon peel; stir until butter melts. Arrange pears in two layers over hot sugar mixture in skillet. Fill open spaces with pear slices; sprinkle with lemon juice. Roll pastry to 10-inch round and place over pears. Bake at 425°F 25 to 30 minutes or until pastry is golden brown. Cool, in pan, 30 minutes. If there seems to be too much sauce in pan, pour excess sauce into 1-pint container and reserve to serve over tart. Invert tart onto shallow serving dish. Serve warm with yogurt. *Makes 6 to 8 servings*

Favorite recipe from **Pear Bureau Northwest**

Upside-Down Pear Tart

Blueberry Streusel Cobbler

1 pint fresh or frozen blueberries
1 (14-ounce) can EAGLE BRAND® Sweetened Condensed Milk (NOT evaporated milk)
2 teaspoons grated lemon peel
¾ cup (1½ sticks) plus 2 tablespoons cold butter or margarine, divided
2 cups biscuit baking mix, divided
½ cup firmly packed light brown sugar
½ cup chopped nuts
Vanilla ice cream
Blueberry Sauce (recipe follows)

1. Preheat oven to 325°F. In medium mixing bowl, combine blueberries, EAGLE BRAND® and lemon peel.

2. In large mixing bowl, cut ¾ cup butter into 1½ cups biscuit mix until crumbly; add blueberry mixture. Spread in greased 9-inch square baking pan.

3. In small mixing bowl, combine remaining ½ cup biscuit mix and brown sugar; cut in remaining 2 tablespoons butter until crumbly. Add nuts. Sprinkle over cobbler.

4. Bake 1 hour and 10 minutes or until golden. Serve warm with vanilla ice cream and Blueberry Sauce. Refrigerate leftovers.

Makes 8 to 12 servings

Blueberry Sauce: In large saucepan over medium heat, combine ½ cup sugar, 1 tablespoon cornstarch, ½ teaspoon ground cinnamon and ¼ teaspoon ground nutmeg. Gradually add ½ cup water. Cook and stir until thickened. Stir in 1 pint blueberries; cook and stir until hot. Makes about 1⅔ cups.

Chocolate Chip Walnut Pie

¾ cup packed light brown sugar
½ cup all-purpose flour
½ teaspoon baking powder
¼ teaspoon ground cinnamon
2 eggs, slightly beaten
1 cup HERSHEY'S MINI CHIPS™ Semi-Sweet Chocolate Chips, HERSHEY'S Semi-Sweet or Milk Chocolate Chips
1 cup coarsely chopped walnuts
1 baked (9-inch) pie crust
Spiced Cream (recipe follows)

1. Heat oven to 350°F.

2. Combine brown sugar, flour, baking powder and cinnamon in medium bowl. Add eggs; stir until well blended. Add chocolate chips and walnuts. Pour into baked pie crust.

3. Bake 25 to 30 minutes or until lightly browned and set. Serve slightly warm or at room temperature with Spiced Cream. Refrigerate leftovers.

Makes 1 (9-inch) pie

Spiced Cream: Combine ½ cup chilled whipping cream, 1 tablespoon powdered sugar, ¼ teaspoon vanilla extract, ¼ teaspoon ground cinnamon and dash ground nutmeg in small bowl; beat until stiff. Makes about 1 cup topping.

Blueberry Streusel Cobbler

Berry Cobbler

1 pint (2½ cups) fresh raspberries*
1 pint (2½ cups) fresh blueberries or strawberries,* sliced
2 tablespoons cornstarch
½ to ¾ cup sugar
1 cup all-purpose flour
1½ teaspoons baking powder
¼ teaspoon salt
⅓ cup milk
⅓ cup butter or margarine, melted
2 tablespoons thawed frozen apple juice concentrate
¼ teaspoon ground nutmeg

**One (16-ounce) bag frozen raspberries and one (16-ounce) bag frozen blueberries or strawberries can be substituted for fresh berries. Thaw berries, reserving juices. Increase cornstarch to 3 tablespoons.*

1. Preheat oven to 375°F.

2. Combine berries and cornstarch in medium bowl; toss lightly to coat. Add sugar to taste; mix well. Spoon into 1½-quart or 8-inch square baking dish. Combine flour, baking powder and salt in medium bowl. Add milk, butter and juice concentrate; mix just until dry ingredients are moistened. Drop 6 heaping tablespoonfuls batter evenly over berries; sprinkle with nutmeg.

3. Bake 25 minutes or until topping is golden brown and fruit is bubbly. Cool on wire rack. Serve warm or at room temperature.

Makes 6 servings

Tip: Cobblers are best served warm or at room temperature on the day they are made. Leftovers should be kept covered and refrigerated for up to two days. Reheat them, covered, in a 350°F oven until warm.

Prep Time: 5 minutes
Bake Time: 25 minutes

Coconut Peach Crunch Pie

1 (6-ounce) READY CRUST® Shortbread Pie Crust
1 egg yolk, beaten
1 (21-ounce) can peach pie filling
1 cup flaked coconut
½ cup all-purpose flour
½ cup sugar
¼ cup wheat germ
¼ cup margarine, melted

1. Preheat oven to 375°F. Brush bottom and sides of crust with egg yolk; bake on baking sheet 5 minutes or until golden brown.

2. Spoon peach filling into crust. Combine coconut, flour, sugar, wheat germ and margarine in small bowl. Mix until well blended. Spread over peach filling.

3. Bake on baking sheet 30 to 35 minutes or until filling is bubbly and topping is light brown. Cool on wire rack. *Makes 8 servings*

Preparation Time: 15 minutes
Baking Time: 35 to 40 minutes

Berry Cobbler

Blueberry Crumble Pie

1 (6-ounce) READY CRUST® Graham Cracker Pie Crust
1 egg yolk, beaten
1 (21-ounce) can blueberry pie filling
⅓ cup all-purpose flour
⅓ cup quick-cooking oats
¼ cup sugar
3 tablespoons margarine, melted

1. Preheat oven to 375°F. Brush bottom and sides of crust with egg yolk; bake on baking sheet 5 minutes or until light brown.

2. Pour blueberry pie filling into crust. Combine flour, oats and sugar in small bowl; mix in margarine. Spoon over pie filling.

3. Bake on baking sheet about 35 minutes or until filling is bubbly and topping is browned. Cool on wire rack. *Makes 8 servings*

Preparation Time: 15 minutes
Baking Time: 40 minutes

Lemon Buttermilk Pie

1 (9-inch) unbaked pie crust*
1½ cups sugar
½ cup (1 stick) butter, softened
3 eggs
1 cup buttermilk
1 tablespoon cornstarch
1 tablespoon fresh lemon juice
⅛ teaspoon salt

**If using a commercial frozen pie crust, purchase a deep-dish crust and thaw before using.*

Heat oven to 350°F. Prick crust all over with fork. Bake until light golden brown, about 8 minutes; cool on wire rack. *Reduce oven temperature to* 325°F. In large bowl, beat sugar and butter until creamy. Add eggs, one at a time, beating well after each addition. Add buttermilk, cornstarch, lemon juice and salt; mix well. Pour filling into crust. Bake 55 to 60 minutes or just until knife inserted near center comes out clean. Cool; cover and chill.

Makes 8 servings

Favorite recipe from **Southeast United Dairy Industry Association, Inc.**

Blueberry Crumble Pie

Blueberry Granola Crumble Pie

1 package (16 ounces) frozen unsweetened blueberries
¼ cup sugar
2 tablespoons lemon juice
1½ tablespoons cornstarch
2 teaspoons vanilla
1 frozen reduced-fat pie crust
1 cup low-fat granola

1. Preheat oven to 425°F. Place baking sheet in oven while preheating.

2. Toss blueberries with sugar, lemon juice, cornstarch and vanilla to coat. Spoon blueberry mixture into pie crust; place on heated baking sheet.

3. Bake 20 minutes; sprinkle granola evenly over pie. Bake an additional 20 minutes or until pie is bubbly. *Makes 8 servings*

Cook's Tip: If pie is allowed to stand 4 hours or overnight, the flavors will blend, making a sweeter-tasting dessert. This is true with most fruit pies, especially blueberry, cherry and peach pies.

Fresh Nectarine-Pineapple Cobbler

1½ cups DOLE® Fresh Pineapple, cut into chunks
3 cups sliced ripe DOLE® Fresh Nectarines or Peaches
½ cup sugar
2 tablespoons all-purpose flour
½ teaspoon ground cinnamon
1 cup buttermilk baking mix
½ cup low-fat milk

- Combine pineapple, nectarines, sugar, flour and cinnamon in 8×8-inch glass baking dish; spread fruit evenly in dish.
- Stir together baking mix and milk in small bowl until just combined. Pour over fruit.
- Bake at 400°F 40 to 45 minutes or until fruit is tender and crust is browned. *Makes 8 servings*

Prep Time: 20 minutes
Bake Time: 45 minutes

Autumn Pear Tart

- Reduced-Fat Pastry (recipe follows)
- 3 to 4 tablespoons sugar
- 2 tablespoons cornstarch
- 3 to 4 large pears, cut into halves, cored, pared and sliced
- 1 tablespoon lemon juice
- Ground cinnamon (optional)
- Ground nutmeg (optional)
- ¼ cup apple jelly, apricot spreadable fruit or honey, warm

1. Preheat oven to 425°F. Roll out pastry on floured surface to ⅛-inch thickness. Ease pastry into 9-inch tart pan with removable bottom; trim edge. Pierce bottom of pastry with tines of fork; bake 15 to 20 minutes or until pastry begins to brown. Cool on wire rack.

2. Combine sugar and cornstarch in small bowl; mix well. Sprinkle pears with lemon juice; toss with sugar mixture. Arrange sliced pears on pastry. Sprinkle lightly with cinnamon and nutmeg, if desired.

3. Bake 20 to 30 minutes or until pears are tender and crust is browned. Cool on wire rack. Brush pears with jelly. Remove side of pan; place tart on serving plate. *Makes 8 servings*

Reduced-Fat Pastry

- 1⅓ cups cake flour
- 2 tablespoons sugar
- ¼ teaspoon salt
- ¼ cup vegetable shortening
- 4 to 5 tablespoons ice water

Combine flour, sugar and salt in small bowl. Cut in shortening with pastry blender or 2 knives until mixture forms coarse crumbs. Mix in ice water, 1 tablespoon at a time, until mixture comes together and forms a soft dough. Wrap in plastic wrap. Refrigerate 30 minutes before using.

Makes pastry for one (9-inch) tart

Fudgy Pecan Pie

¼ cup (½ stick) butter or margarine
2 (1-ounce) squares unsweetened chocolate
1 (14-ounce) can EAGLE BRAND® Sweetened Condensed Milk (NOT evaporated milk)
½ cup hot water
2 eggs, well beaten
1¼ cups pecan halves or pieces
1 teaspoon vanilla extract
⅛ teaspoon salt
1 (9-inch) unbaked pie crust

1. Preheat oven to 350°F. In medium saucepan over low heat, melt butter and chocolate. Stir in EAGLE BRAND®, hot water and eggs; mix well.

2. Remove from heat; stir in pecans, vanilla and salt. Pour into pie crust. Bake 40 to 45 minutes or until center is set. Cool slightly. Serve warm or chilled. Garnish as desired. Store covered in refrigerator. *Makes one 9-inch pie*

Prep Time: 15 minutes
Bake Time: 40 to 45 minutes

Traditional Cherry Pie

4 cups frozen tart cherries*
1⅓ cups granulated sugar
3 tablespoons quick-cooking tapioca or cornstarch
½ teaspoon almond extract
Pastry for double crust 9-inch pie
2 tablespoons butter or margarine

**It is not necessary to thaw cherries before using.*

In medium bowl, combine cherries, sugar, tapioca and almond extract; mix well. Let cherry mixture stand 15 minutes.

Line 9-inch pie plate with pastry; fill with cherry mixture. Dot with butter. Cover with top crust; cut slits for steam to escape.

Bake in preheated 400°F oven 50 to 55 minutes or until crust is golden brown and filling is bubbly.

Makes 6 to 8 servings

Favorite recipe from **Cherry Marketing Institute**

Quick Tip

Tapioca is used both as a thickener, particularly for fruit pies, and as a creamy dessert pudding. It is good for foods that will be frozen, because freezing and thawing do not affect its thickening properties.

Fudgy Pecan Pie

White Chocolate Cranberry Tart

1 refrigerated pie crust (half of 15-ounce package)
1 cup sugar
2 eggs
¼ cup (½ stick) butter, melted
2 teaspoons vanilla
½ cup all-purpose flour
6 squares (1 ounce each) white chocolate, chopped
½ cup chopped macadamia nuts, lightly toasted*
½ cup dried cranberries, coarsely chopped

**Toast chopped macadamia nuts in hot skillet over medium heat about 3 minutes or until fragrant.*

1. Preheat oven to 350°F. Place pie crust in 9-inch tart pan with removable bottom or pie pan. (Refrigerate or freeze other crust for another use.)

2. Combine sugar, eggs, butter and vanilla in large bowl; mix well. Stir in flour until well blended. Add white chocolate, nuts and cranberries.

3. Pour filling into unbaked crust. Bake 50 to 55 minutes or until top of tart is crusty and deep golden brown and knife inserted into center comes out clean.

4. Cool completely on wire rack.

Makes 8 servings

Serve it with Style!: Top each serving with a dollop of whipped cream flavored with ground cinnamon, a favorite liqueur and grated orange peel.

Make-Ahead Time: up to 2 days before serving

Spiced Cranberry-Apple Sour Cream Cobbler

4 cups cranberries, washed
6 Granny Smith apples, peeled and thinly sliced
2 cups firmly packed light brown sugar
1 teaspoon ground cinnamon
1 teaspoon vanilla
¼ teaspoon ground cloves
2 cups plus 1 tablespoon all-purpose flour, divided
¼ cup (½ stick) butter, cut into pieces
2 teaspoons double acting baking powder
1 teaspoon salt
½ CRISCO® Stick or ½ cup CRISCO® all-vegetable shortening
1½ cups sour cream
2 teaspoons granulated sugar
Cinnamon or vanilla ice cream

1. Heat oven to 400°F. Combine cranberries, apples, brown sugar, cinnamon, vanilla, ground cloves and 1 tablespoon flour in 3-quart baking dish; mix evenly. Dot top with butter.

2. Stir together remaining 2 cups flour, baking powder and salt in medium bowl. Cut in ½ cup shortening using pastry blender or 2 knives until medium-size crumbs form. Add sour cream; blend well. (Dough will be sticky.) Drop dough by spoonfuls on top of fruit mixture. Sprinkle with granulated sugar. Bake at 400°F for 20 to 30 minutes, on middle rack, until top is golden. Serve with cinnamon or vanilla ice cream, if desired.

Makes 6 to 8 servings

Kitchen Hint: Lucky enough to have some leftover cobbler? Store it in the refrigerator for up to two days. Reheat it, covered, in a 350°F oven until warm.

White Chocolate Cranberry Tart

Spicy Raisin, Date & Candied Ginger Cobbler

- ⅔ cup granulated sugar
- 2 tablespoons cornstarch
- 2 cups seedless raisins
- 1 cup pitted dates, chopped
- 1 cup orange juice
- ⅓ cup water
- 2 tablespoons finely chopped candied ginger
- 3 tablespoons butter, divided
- 1 tablespoon lemon juice
- ½ teaspoon salt
- 1 small seedless orange, peeled, quartered and thinly sliced
- 1 can (10 ounces) flaky biscuits
- 2 tablespoons brown sugar
- Whipped cream (optional)

1. Preheat oven to 450°F. Combine granulated sugar and cornstarch in large saucepan. Stir in raisins, dates, orange juice, water and ginger. Bring to a simmer over medium heat, stirring constantly, until liquid is just thickened. Remove from heat. Stir in 1 tablespoon butter, lemon juice and salt. Fold in orange slices. Pour into 2-quart casserole dish.

2. Split biscuits horizontally in half. Cover top of raisin mixture with biscuit halves. Melt remaining 2 tablespoons butter. Brush butter onto biscuits. Sprinkle biscuits with brown sugar. Bake 10 minutes. *Reduce oven temperature to* 350°F; bake 15 to 20 minutes or until biscuits are golden brown. Cool on wire rack. Serve warm or at room temperature with whipped cream, if desired.

Makes 8 to 10 servings

Country Fruit Pie

- 2 pie crust sticks
- 5 fresh California peaches or nectarines, each cut into 8 slices (about 3 cups)
- 3 fresh California plums, each cut into 6 slices (about 1 cup)
- ⅓ cup honey
- 3 tablespoons all-purpose flour
- ½ teaspoon almond extract

Preheat oven to 400°F. Roll out 1 pie crust stick according to package directions to fit 8-inch pie dish. Roll out remaining pie crust stick; cut out about 35 leaf shapes with small leaf-shaped cutter. Gently toss fruit, honey, flour and almond extract in large bowl. Spoon fruit mixture into crust. Place 8 leaf cut-outs over fruit; press remaining leaves onto rim of pie crust with small amount of water. Bake 25 to 30 minutes or until crust is browned and fruit is easily pierced with knife.

Makes 8 servings

Favorite recipe from **California Tree Fruit Agreement**

Spicy Raisin, Date & Candied Ginger Cobbler

Honey Pumpkin Pie

1 can (16 ounces) solid pack pumpkin
1 cup evaporated low-fat milk
¾ cup honey
3 eggs, slightly beaten
2 tablespoons all-purpose flour
1 teaspoon ground cinnamon
½ teaspoon ground ginger
½ teaspoon rum extract
Pastry for single 9-inch pie crust

Combine all ingredients except pastry in large bowl; beat until well blended. Pour into pastry-lined 9-inch pie plate. Bake at 400°F 45 minutes or until knife inserted near center comes out clean. *Makes 8 servings*

Favorite recipe from **National Honey Board**

Quick Tip

Extracts are very concentrated flavorings derived from a variety of foods. Small amounts, usually a teaspoon or less, provide a lot of flavor impact without adding any volume or moisture. A wide variety of extracts and flavorings are available in the spice section of the supermarket. A basic kitchen pantry should have vanilla, almond and lemon extracts. Extracts are sensitive to heat and light. To prevent evaporation and loss of flavor, keep bottles tightly closed and stored in a cool, dark place.

Reese's® Peanut Butter and Milk Chocolate Chip Cookie Pie

½ cup (1 stick) butter or margarine, softened
2 eggs, beaten
2 teaspoons vanilla extract
1 cup sugar
½ cup all-purpose flour
1¾ cups (11-ounce package) REESE'S® Peanut Butter and Milk Chocolate Chips
1 cup chopped pecans or walnuts
1 unbaked 9-inch pie crust
Sweetened whipped cream or ice cream (optional)

1. Heat oven to 350°F.

2. Beat butter in medium bowl; add eggs and vanilla. Stir together sugar and flour; add to butter mixture. Stir in chips and nuts; pour into unbaked pie crust.

3. Bake 50 to 55 minutes or until golden brown. Cool about 1 hour on wire rack; serve warm with sweetened whipped cream or ice cream, if desired. To reheat: Microwave one slice at a time at HIGH (100%) 10 to 15 seconds.

Makes 8 to 10 servings

Honey Pumpkin Pie

Fresh Lemon Meringue Pie

1½ cups sugar
¼ cup plus 2 tablespoons cornstarch
½ teaspoon salt
½ cup cold water
½ cup freshly squeezed SUNKIST® lemon juice
3 egg yolks, well beaten
2 tablespoons butter or margarine
1½ cups boiling water
Grated peel of ½ SUNKIST® lemon
2 to 3 drops yellow food coloring (optional)
1 (9-inch) baked pie crust
Three-Egg Meringue (recipe follows)

In large saucepan, combine sugar, cornstarch and salt. Gradually blend in cold water and lemon juice. Stir in egg yolks. Add butter and boiling water. Bring to a boil over medium-high heat, stirring constantly. Reduce heat to medium and boil 1 minute. Remove from heat; stir in lemon peel and food coloring. Pour into baked pie crust. Top with Three-Egg Meringue, sealing well at edges. Bake at 350°F 12 to 15 minutes. Cool 2 hours before serving. *Makes 6 servings*

Three-Egg Meringue

3 egg whites
¼ teaspoon cream of tartar
6 tablespoons sugar

**Use clean, uncracked Grade A eggs.*

In large bowl with electric mixer, beat egg whites with cream of tartar until foamy. Gradually add sugar and beat until stiff peaks form.

Cherry Apricot Cornmeal Cobbler

2 cups sliced pitted halved fresh apricots
⅓ cup granulated sugar
2 cups pitted fresh cherries
1 cup plus 1 tablespoon all-purpose flour, divided
½ cup yellow cornmeal
½ teaspoon ground cinnamon
¼ teaspoon salt
1½ tablespoons plus 1 teaspoon brown sugar, divided
2 teaspoons baking powder
5 tablespoons margarine
¾ cup low-fat milk

1. Preheat oven to 375°F. Combine apricots and granulated sugar in small bowl. Combine cherries and 1 tablespoon flour in second bowl; set aside. Combine remaining 1 cup flour, cornmeal, cinnamon, salt, 1½ tablespoons brown sugar and baking powder in large bowl. Cut in margarine until mixture resembles coarse crumbs. Add milk; blend just until ingredients are evenly moistened.

2. Place fruit in 1½-quart baking dish; top with batter. Sprinkle with remaining 1 teaspoon brown sugar. Bake 25 to 30 minutes or until golden brown. Let cool slightly before serving.

Makes 8 servings

Fresh Lemon Meringue Pie

Country Pecan Pie

Pie pastry for single 9-inch pie crust
1¼ cups dark corn syrup
4 eggs
½ cup packed light brown sugar
¼ cup (½ stick) butter or margarine, melted
2 teaspoons all-purpose flour
1½ teaspoons vanilla
1½ cups pecan halves

1. Preheat oven to 350°F. Roll pastry on lightly floured surface to form 13-inch circle. Fit into 9-inch pie plate. Trim edges; flute. Set aside.

2. Combine corn syrup, eggs, brown sugar and melted butter in large bowl; beat with electric mixer on medium speed until well blended. Stir in flour and vanilla until blended. Pour into unbaked pie crust. Arrange pecans on top.

3. Bake 40 to 45 minutes until center of filling is puffed and golden brown. Cool completely on wire rack. Garnish as desired.

Makes one 9-inch pie

Rhubarb Tart

Pastry for single-crust 9-inch pie
4 cups sliced (½-inch pieces) fresh rhubarb
1¼ cups sugar
¼ cup all-purpose flour
2 tablespoons butter, cut into chunks
¼ cup uncooked old-fashioned oats

1. Preheat oven to 450°F. Line 9-inch pie plate with pastry; set aside.

2. Combine rhubarb, sugar and flour in medium bowl; place in pie crust. Top with butter. Sprinkle with oats.

3. Bake 10 minutes. *Reduce oven temperature to* 350°F. Bake 40 minutes more or until bubbly.

Makes 8 servings

Quick Tip

Store rhubarb in the refrigerator in a plastic bag. It will keep for about three to five days. Cleaned and dried rhubarb stalks can be cut into 1-inch pieces and frozen in a plastic freezer bag for up to nine months.

Country Pecan Pie

Blueberry-Pear Tart

- 1 refrigerated pie crust dough
- 1 (8-ounce) fully ripened pear, peeled, cored and thinly sliced
- 8 ounces fresh or thawed frozen blueberries or blackberries
- ⅓ cup no-sugar-added raspberry fruit spread
- ½ teaspoon grated gingerroot

1. Preheat oven to 450°F.

2. Spray 9-inch tart pan with nonstick cooking spray. Place dough in pan; press against side of pan to form ½-inch edge. Prick dough with fork. Bake 12 minutes. Remove pan to wire rack; cool completely.

3. Arrange pears on bottom of cooled crust; top with blueberries.

4. Place fruit spread in small microwavable bowl. Cover with plastic wrap; microwave at HIGH 15 seconds; stir. If necessary, microwave additional 10 to 15 seconds or until spread is melted; stir. Add grated ginger; stir until blended. Let stand 30 seconds to thicken slightly. Pour mixture over fruit in crust. Refrigerate 2 hours. (Do not cover.) Cut into 8 slices before serving.

Makes 8 servings

Prep Time: 10 minutes
Bake Time: 12 minutes
Chill Time: 2 hours

Sweet Potato Pie

- 2 eggs
- 1 can (15 ounces) PRINCELLA® or SUGARY SAM® Cut Sweet Potatoes, drained
- 1 can (12 ounces) evaporated milk
- ¾ cup sugar
- 1 teaspoon ground cinnamon
- ½ teaspoon ground ginger
- ¼ teaspoon ground cloves
- 1 unbaked 9-inch pie crust

Preheat oven to 425°F. In large mixing bowl, beat eggs. Add sweet potatoes and mix with an electric hand mixer for 3 minutes until very smooth. Stir in evaporated milk and mix 2 minutes or until well blended. Add sugar, cinnamon, ginger and cloves; mix well. Pour mixture into pie crust and bake 15 minutes. Reduce temperature to 350°F and bake 40 to 50 minutes or until knife inserted near center comes out clean. Cool for 2 hours. Serve immediately or refrigerate. *Makes 8 servings*

Tasty Tip: Serve with whipped topping or vanilla ice cream.

Blueberry-Pear Tart

Fabulous Fruit Tart

Pastry for single-crust 9-inch pie
1 package (8 ounces) reduced-fat cream cheese, softened
⅓ cup no-sugar-added raspberry fruit spread
½ cup sliced peaches or nectarines*
⅓ cup sliced strawberries*
½ cup kiwifruit slices*
⅓ cup raspberries*
3 tablespoons no-sugar-added apricot pourable fruit**
2 teaspoons raspberry-flavored liqueur (optional)

**Sliced bananas, plums or blueberries can be substituted.*

***2 tablespoons no-sugar-added apricot fruit spread combined with 1 tablespoon warm water can be substituted.*

1. Preheat oven to 350°F. Roll out pastry to 12-inch circle; place in 10-inch tart pan with removable bottom or 10-inch quiche dish. Prick bottom and sides of pastry with fork. Bake 18 to 20 minutes or until golden brown. Cool completely on wire rack.

2. Combine cream cheese and fruit spread; mix well. Spread onto bottom of cooled pastry. Chill at least 1 hour. Just before serving, arrange fruit over cream cheese layer. Combine pourable fruit and liqueur, if desired; brush evenly over fruit.

Makes 8 servings

Quaker's Best Oatmeal Pie

6 egg whites, lightly beaten *or* ¾ cup egg substitute
⅔ cup firmly packed brown sugar
⅓ cup granulated sugar
¾ cup fat-free milk
1 teaspoon vanilla
1¼ cups QUAKER® Oats (quick or old fashioned, uncooked)
¾ cup raisins or other dried fruit such as cherries, cranberries or chopped apricots
½ cup flaked or shredded coconut
½ cup chopped nuts (optional)
1 prepared 9-inch pie crust, unbaked

Heat oven to 375°F. Beat egg whites and sugars until well blended. Add milk and vanilla; mix well. Stir in oats, raisins, coconut and nuts; mix well. Pour filling into prepared pie crust. Bake 35 to 45 minutes or until center of pie is set. Cool completely on wire rack. Serve with ice cream or whipped cream. Store, covered, in refrigerator.

Makes 8 servings

Fabulous Fruit Tart

Pumpkin Apple Tart

Crust

1 cup plain dry bread crumbs
1 cup crunchy nut-like cereal nuggets
½ cup sugar
½ teaspoon ground cinnamon
½ teaspoon ground nutmeg
¼ cup MOTT'S® Natural Apple Sauce
2 tablespoons margarine, melted
1 egg white

Filling

12 ounces evaporated skim milk
1½ cups solid-pack pumpkin
⅔ cup sugar
½ cup MOTT'S® Chunky Apple Sauce
⅓ cup GRANDMA'S® Molasses
2 egg whites
1 whole egg
½ teaspoon ground ginger
½ teaspoon ground cinnamon
½ teaspoon ground nutmeg
Frozen light nondairy whipped topping, thawed (optional)

1. Preheat oven to 375°F. Spray 9- or 10-inch springform pan with nonstick cooking spray.

2. To prepare Crust, in medium bowl, combine bread crumbs, cereal, ½ cup sugar, ½ teaspoon cinnamon and ½ teaspoon nutmeg.

3. Add ¼ cup apple sauce, margarine and egg white; mix until moistened. Press onto bottom of prepared pan.

4. Bake 8 minutes.

5. To prepare Filling, place evaporated milk in small saucepan. Cook over medium heat until milk almost boils, stirring occasionally.

6. In large bowl, combine evaporated milk, pumpkin, ⅔ cup sugar, ½ cup chunky apple sauce, molasses, 2 egg whites, whole egg, ginger, ½ teaspoon cinnamon and ½ teaspoon nutmeg. Pour into baked crust.

7. Increase oven temperature to 400°F. Bake 35 to 40 minutes or until center is set.

8. Cool 20 minutes on wire rack. Remove side of pan. Spoon or pipe whipped topping onto tart, if desired. Cut into 12 slices. Refrigerate leftovers.

Makes 12 servings

A springform pan is a two-piece round baking pan with an expandable side (secured by a clamp or spring) and a removable bottom. When the clamp is opened, the rim expands and the bottom of the pan can be removed. This makes it easy to remove tarts, cheesecakes, cake and tortes from the pan. The diameter ranges from 4 to 12 inches with 9- to 10-inch pans being the most common.

Pumpkin Apple Tart

Cranberry Cobbler

2 cans (16 ounces each) sliced peaches in light syrup, drained
1 can (16 ounces) whole berry cranberry sauce
1 package DUNCAN HINES® Cinnamon Swirl Muffin Mix
½ cup chopped pecans
⅓ cup butter or margarine, melted
Whipped topping or ice cream

1. Preheat oven to 350°F.

2. Cut peach slices in half lengthwise. Combine peach slices and cranberry sauce in *ungreased* 9-inch square pan. Knead swirl packet from Mix for 10 seconds. Squeeze contents evenly over fruit.

3. Combine muffin mix, contents of topping packet from Mix and pecans in large bowl. Add melted butter. Stir until thoroughly blended (mixture will be crumbly). Sprinkle crumbs over fruit. Bake 40 to 45 minutes or until lightly browned and bubbly. Serve warm with whipped topping. *Makes 9 servings*

Tip: Store leftovers in the refrigerator. Reheat in microwave oven to serve warm.

Apple Crunch Pie

1 refrigerated pie crust (½ of 15-ounce package)
1¼ cups all-purpose flour, divided
1 cup granulated sugar
6 tablespoons butter, melted and divided
1½ teaspoons ground cinnamon, divided
¾ teaspoon ground nutmeg, divided
½ teaspoon ground ginger
¼ teaspoon salt
4 cups peeled, cored, diced apples
½ cup packed brown sugar
½ cup chopped walnuts

1. Preheat oven to 350°F. Place crust in 9-inch pie pan; flute edge as desired.

2. Combine ¼ cup flour, granulated sugar, 2 tablespoons butter, 1 teaspoon cinnamon, ½ teaspoon nutmeg, ginger and salt; mix well. Add apples; toss to coat. Place apple mixture in crust.

3. Combine remaining 1 cup flour, 4 tablespoons butter, ½ teaspoon cinnamon, ¼ teaspoon nutmeg, brown sugar and walnuts in small bowl. Sprinkle evenly over apple mixture.

4. Bake 45 to 55 minutes or until apples are tender. *Makes 8 servings*

Cranberry Cobbler

Acknowledgments

The publisher would like to thank the companies and organizations listed below for the use of their recipes and photographs in this publication.

Allen Canning Company
Arm & Hammer Division, Church & Dwight Co., Inc.
Birds Eye® Foods
California Tree Fruit Agreement
Cherry Marketing Institute
Crisco is a registered trademark of The J.M. Smucker Company
Del Monte Corporation
Dole Food Company, Inc.
Duncan Hines® and Moist Deluxe® are registered trademarks of Pinnacle Foods Corp.
Eagle Brand® Sweetened Condensed Milk
Grandma's® is a registered trademark of Mott's, LLP
Hershey Foods Corporation
The Hidden Valley® Food Products Company
Keebler® Company
© Mars, Incorporated 2005
McIlhenny Company (TABASCO® brand Pepper Sauce)
Mott's® is a registered trademark of Mott's, LLP
National Honey Board
Nestlé USA
Peanut Advisory Board
Pear Bureau Northwest
The Quaker® Oatmeal Kitchens
RED STAR® Yeast, a product of Lasaffre Yeast Corporation
Smucker's® trademark of The J.M. Smucker Company
Southeast United Dairy Industry Association, Inc.
The Sugar Association, Inc.
Reprinted with permission of Sunkist Growers, Inc.
Unilever Foods North America
Walnut Marketing Board
Washington Apple Commission
Wisconsin Milk Marketing Board

METRIC CONVERSION CHART

VOLUME MEASUREMENTS (dry)

1/8 teaspoon = 0.5 mL
1/4 teaspoon = 1 mL
1/2 teaspoon = 2 mL
3/4 teaspoon = 4 mL
1 teaspoon = 5 mL
1 tablespoon = 15 mL
2 tablespoons = 30 mL
1/4 cup = 60 mL
1/3 cup = 75 mL
1/2 cup = 125 mL
2/3 cup = 150 mL
3/4 cup = 175 mL
1 cup = 250 mL
2 cups = 1 pint = 500 mL
3 cups = 750 mL
4 cups = 1 quart = 1 L

VOLUME MEASUREMENTS (fluid)

1 fluid ounce (2 tablespoons) = 30 mL
4 fluid ounces (1/2 cup) = 125 mL
8 fluid ounces (1 cup) = 250 mL
12 fluid ounces (1 1/2 cups) = 375 mL
16 fluid ounces (2 cups) = 500 mL

WEIGHTS (mass)

1/2 ounce = 15 g
1 ounce = 30 g
3 ounces = 90 g
4 ounces = 120 g
8 ounces = 225 g
10 ounces = 285 g
12 ounces = 360 g
16 ounces = 1 pound = 450 g

DIMENSIONS

1/16 inch = 2 mm
1/8 inch = 3 mm
1/4 inch = 6 mm
1/2 inch = 1.5 cm
3/4 inch = 2 cm
1 inch = 2.5 cm

OVEN TEMPERATURES

250°F = 120°C
275°F = 140°C
300°F = 150°C
325°F = 160°C
350°F = 180°C
375°F = 190°C
400°F = 200°C
425°F = 220°C
450°F = 230°C

BAKING PAN SIZES

Utensil	Size in Inches/Quarts	Metric Volume	Size in Centimeters
Baking or Cake Pan (square or rectangular)	8×8×2	2 L	20×20×5
	9×9×2	2.5 L	23×23×5
	12×8×2	3 L	30×20×5
	13×9×2	3.5 L	33×23×5
Loaf Pan	8×4×3	1.5 L	20×10×7
	9×5×3	2 L	23×13×7
Round Layer Cake Pan	8×1½	1.2 L	20×4
	9×1½	1.5 L	23×4
Pie Plate	8×1¼	750 mL	20×3
	9×1¼	1 L	23×3
Baking Dish or Casserole	1 quart	1 L	—
	1½ quart	1.5 L	—
	2 quart	2 L	—